Theory and Personality

Theory and Personality

The Significance of
T. S. Eliot's Criticism

by

BRIAN LEE

... I did not realise at the time of writing how deeply interpretation was rooted in the need to reconcile past and present, letter and spirit, self and other ...

Geoffrey Hartman

LONDON
THE ATHLONE PRESS
1979

Published by
THE ATHLONE PRESS
at 90-91 Great Russell Street, London WC1

Distributed by Tiptree Book Services Ltd
Tiptree, Essex

U.S.A. and Canada
Humanities Press Inc
New Jersey

British Library Cataloguing in Publication Data
Lee, Brian
1. Eliot, Thomas Stearns—Criticism and
interpretation
I. Title
820′.9   PS3509.L43Z
ISBN 0 485 11185 3

Set in Monotype Bembo by
GLOUCESTER TYPESETTING CO LTD
Gloucester

Printed in Great Britain by
EBENEZER BAYLIS & SON LTD
The Trinity Press Worcester and London

For Duke Maskell, and Carol Maskell

ACKNOWLEDGEMENTS

In addition to the general debt acknowledged in the dedication, I owe particular thanks to Professor W. W. Robson (under whose tutorship at Edinburgh University a good deal of the work on this essay was done) for many helpful suggestions as well as fruitful disagreements; to MacDonald Emslie, of the same department; and to Michael MacDowell, a student-colleague, with whom I talked much of it over. Professor Robson and Mr A. D. Moody, of York University suggested the improvement made by the prefatory section. Parts of the essay were given in the form of a talk to members of the English Department of Swansea University, and I am grateful to Ian Robinson for the invitation and the argument that ensued.

CONTENTS

. . . When there is economy of effort it is possible to have several, even many, good poets at once. The great ages did not perhaps *produce* much more talent than ours, but less talent was wasted. Now in a formless age there is very little hope for the minor poet to do anything worth doing . . . under the present conditions, the minor poet has too much to do . . .

T. S. Eliot, 'The Possibility of a Poetic Drama' in *The Sacred Wood*, p. 64

. . . his own personality . . . groped through the war-crumbled world towards possession of itself in the shape of conviction, resoluteness and weight.

Paul Rosenfeld, of D. H. Lawrence, *Men Seen*, 1925

Eliot's Four 'Theories'

Eliot was a critic of his own criticism sometimes to the point of 'disparagement for no very obvious reason'.[1] And we are the critics of the critic-of-the-critic. We find new facts and information and new things to say; we agree, and we disagree—and this is our reason for continuing to criticize, in the common pursuit of true judgment. In Eliot's case the pursuit has a special difficulty: he presents us with a problem different from that of Arnold, or Wordsworth or even Coleridge (though the latter's definitions of Imagination and Fancy have given a similar difficulty). We cannot accept what he says and argue over whether it is right or not —we have first of all to decide what he means. Whatever our 'approach', that is where a great deal of the difficulty of interpretation has lain. How do we square *this* remark with *that*? How do these words connect? How do the four theories fit together? This contradicts that—or does it, *really*?

Hence, there has been a great deal of useful accumulation of information-about—'background'—and much useful activity of explication and connection. We find that sense *is* made. But nevertheless the contradictions are there, before us, on the page, and will always stay there for new readers who read him, as they should, before they read us. At some point someone must ask: Why are they there? Why did Eliot leave them there? What does it mean? There does seem to be something more to be said.

The purpose of this particular bit of more-saying is to try to offer an explanation of what it does mean, through a simple but close reading of the essays, and by a concentration of attention upon two central terms, expressive of a central interest: Impersonality and Personality. As it is an interpretation it is a study of *words in use*, an attempt to extract as much of the juice of significance from them as may be. So, even if one had hoped to do so, it would not have been possible to abstract the terms from the text and place them in an expository relation to those other 'key-words' of Eliot's brief 'theories': *tradition*, the *objective correlative*, *dissociation of sensibility*. Here, something is offered, more detailed and less 'theoretical' in itself, less theoretical even than what is proposed *here*:

> we have to know something of the epistemological system, the terms of which control the terms of Eliot's literary criticism; we have, in short, to be sensitive to the philosophical nuances of words like 'object', 'feeling', 'ideas', 'point of view' as Eliot uses them. It is somewhat surprising that many expositors of Eliot who would not think of interpreting what Aristotle means by 'mimesis' apart from his other writings and apart from his frame of reference, or what Coleridge means by 'imagination' apart from his total effort as poet and theorist, have ventured to show what Eliot means by these terms without putting them into a fairly complicated context. But Eliot, of course, has been a somewhat indifferent parent to his critical ideas, leaving them like infants on various doorsteps, allowing other people to raise them, and acknowledging only those whose faces make up well.[2]

This is a good statement of part of the necessity; but the context required is still a context of 'ideas', although Mr Thompson has stepped back from theory to the suggestion that 'literary criticism is probably like theology' where 'the basic statements are figurative'. The context I wish to provide is not one of ideas, but merely one of words.

The four chapters that follow are neither theology nor theory; nor are they even expository. Their purpose is largely to question whether certain things about Eliot's criticism can be understood if one begins with the expectations or the methods of an expositor, exegeticist, or theoretic critic. Hence the first chapter. Certain other things can be—but not everything. It is possible, in the words of Mrs Gradgrind, that there may be something which 'all our Ologies' (or Isms) have left out. In concentrating on just two words, and in spending so much time on detailed examination of 'Tradition and the Individual Talent' (regarded still as a master-piece:

... Wordsworth was only thirty-one when he wrote the famous Preface, and Eliot must have been exactly the same age (thirty or thirty-one) when he completed 'Tradition and the Individual Talent'. The coincidence is striking, but what I find even more significant is the composition of their critical masterpieces when they were still so comparatively young.)[3]

perhaps one will be able to point to something that has been left out, with some of its significance and some of the significance of leaving it out.

Of course it is not possible to feel ungrateful for the gradual accretion of information since Matthiessen and earlier. There is now a general understanding (imperfectly expressed perhaps in any one place) about 'what Eliot meant to say'[4] in his criticism: the separated 'theories' within the separate contexts of their essays have been linked with one another and with the two theoretic essays, 'Tradition and the Individual Talent', and 'The Function of Criticism', and beyond to the historical context of ideas. Eliot's eclectic and assimilative critical temperament has had its substructure reconstructed. And in order for the subsequent argument to have *its* context too, it is best here to try to make use of our present understanding to present the word *Impersonality* in its context as it might be by an expository critic.

The main thing such a critic has to do is connect what is disconnected; for if there is one curious characteristic of Eliot's criticism, it is his *apparent* carelessness about making the connections himself: he *is* an indifferent parent. He does not answer our obvious question: How do these things fit together?:

To ask what this cricitism means is to ask two questions. What did the poet write it for? and what 'idea' explains and reconciles puzzling and seemingly discrepant utterances?[5]

We try to answer a question Eliot might have answered himself. And once we have put together an answer there is another question to be asked.

The full extent of the problem for which Eliot was trying to find an answer in his criticism is indicated in the epigraph: how to be a poet in a world where all depth has shrunk. The problem is a crisis—which I. A. Richards tried to deal with in *Science and*

Poetry, which Nietzsche stated in *The Birth of Tragedy*: 'Man today, stripped of myth, stands famished among all his pasts . . .'. It is the Waste Land. Even there, poets must still try and write poetry, try and explain to themselves why it is so hard, and find ways to write as well as they can, or they are not alive in their own natures. The difficulty of the situation in part accounts for Eliot's sense of effort. In 'Tradition and the Individual Talent' he speaks, of the sense of tradition only being 'obtained by great labour' and in 'The Perfect Critic' he says:

> The end of the enjoyment of poetry is a pure contemplation from which all the accidents of personal emotion are removed; thus we aim to see the object as it really is and find a meaning for the words of Arnold. And without a labour which is largely a labour of the intelligence, we are unable to attain that stage of vision *amor intellectualis Dei*.[6]

Eliot hoped for such a transcendence, but he did not disguise the effort from himself. The transcendence would be impersonal in the sense that it would be a triumph—paradoxically—over social circumstance and therefore at the same time, a triumph over personal circumstance; over the times which are a part of the self, but are not the whole of the self.

The criticism is the labour—a labour for his own nature as a poet; and in that it is not something which poets have always had to undertake (when poetry is easier to write, so is criticism), it is in itself another sign of the times. What is wrong? What has gone wrong? How can it be put to rights? Any serious writer, one who is likely to count, has to put those questions to himself. It was Eliot himself who remarked that of two poets with more or less equal talent, the one most likely to turn out lasting work will be the one who is most critical.

The struggle for intelligence was a struggle for critical intelligence, for critical intelligence in poetry—*not* an intelligence which is specialized. Here Eliot was helped to define what he thought by the presence of Arnold's pro-romantic criticism: he came to feel that the fatal weakness in Romantic poetry was not a lack of 'genius' (he thought that one age was likely to produce as much talent as another) but a lack of the intelligence which he identified as 'wit' (a kind of critical poise) in the Metaphysical poets. By his

own time the weakness—the development of a still earlier flaw—
had come to be something much more serious: the Romantic
confidence in the self had degenerated to a corrupt self-expression,
which Eliot denoted by the word 'personality', and against which
he in turn set his word 'impersonality'. It is the relation between
these words (they react and reciprocate with one another, and
with other words which are important in Eliot's vocabulary) that
is the subject of the following four chapters.

The corruption of 'personality' is one of the consequences of
the 'dissociation of sensibility'. In this 'theory' Eliot tries to explain
what has gone wrong: over two centuries and a half thought and
feeling have separated so far that thought has to undertake a
surgical operation upon itself—and upon feeling. It is a case of the
wounded surgeon plying the steel which questions a dis-
tempered part. (Eliot's metaphors—see below, pages 99–100—are
frequently surgical-medical: it tells us a little about how he saw
himself.) The cure is bound up with the sickness, but the aetiology
can be seen. Eliot's 'theory of dissociation', despite its acuteness, is
characteristically incomplete:

> The difference . . . is *something which had happened* to the mind
> of England between the time of Donne or Lord Herbert of
> Cherbury and the time of Tennyson and Browning; it is the
> difference between the intellectual poet and the reflective poet
> . . . We may express the difference by the following theory:
> . . . In the seventeenth century a dissociation of sensibility *set in*,
> from which we have never recovered . . . (my italics).[7]

'Something . . . set in.' The question what? has had answers since,
from L. C. Knights, S. L. Bethell, L. I. Bredvold, Donald Davie
and of course F. R. Leavis; but Eliot's own insight (which it
should be one of the principal tasks of the criticism of the present
to insist on the recognition of) does not instigate the search for an
answer himself. Presumably he felt that he knew enough for his
purposes and so he provides only a sketch, but concentrated to the
point of poetry: Tennyson and Browning do not feel thought
'as immediately as the odour of a rose', whereas for Donne a
thought was an experience and it modified his sensibility; he becomes the exemplar of the poetic mind which—unlike that of
'ordinary men'—can form new wholes from things as different

2

as falling in love, reading Spinoza, the noise of a typewriter or the smell of cooking. In his critical act Eliot recreates his sense of Donne's value—and almost performs the trick himself—but what has happened to the mind of England since Shakespeare? 'A mechanism of sensibility which could devour any kind of experience' (another organic-mechanical metaphor) became the victim of a dissociation. This was 'aggravated' by Milton and Dryden; in the eighteenth century there was a refinement of language in a certain direction while in another direction the feeling became more crude. The sentimental age succeeded. Poets in the romantic period revolted against the ratiocinative eighteenth century only to think and feel by fits, unbalanced. They reflected; Browning and Tennyson ruminated. There Eliot stops, without mentioning Swinburne, who in *The Sacred Wood* had been his example of a poet where sound and sense were more separated than ever before in poetry of such quality. If recovery is possible it must be in the poetry of Eliot and Pound. Eliot had to have that hope: recovery would be transcendence.

The logic of Eliot's position was inescapable: without confidence in his own individual talent he could not hope to escape from the circumstances he depicts: but the radical advance of dissociation as he himself expresses it implicates him, though he does not directly say so. He has to try to create his own confidence with what help he can find. He was fortunate in Pound; and for near-contemporary sustenance, in criticism, and for something corresponding to 'wit' he looked to France—to Corbière, Laforgue, Valéry, de Gourmont, to *l'intélligence* (not *our* intelligence) and the tradition of *la clarté*.

His other resource was to a conception of *tradition*, which I shall consider here as one variety of Impersonality. Eliot implies so much, though he does not say so with absolute explicitness: 'The other aspect of this Impersonal theory of poetry is the relation of the poem to its author.'[8] This is the way in which Eliot joins the two parts of 'Tradition and the Individual Talent', where the 'theory' of Impersonality follows the exposition of Tradition. The word Impersonality does not occur in part I. In the version of impersonality which is tradition, the poet achieves the former by a 'procuring of the consciousness of the past . . . by great labour'; although some 'can absorb knowledge the more tardy must

sweat for it'. The individual talent measures itself against the existing tradition, the measuring being a form of understanding. That
understanding Eliot himself expresses in his individual judgments
about different poets and dramatists, and by his own 'theory of
dissociation':

> The existing order is complete before the new work arrives;
> for order to persist after the supervention of novelty, the *whole*
> existing order must be, if ever so slightly, altered; and so the
> relations, proportions, values of each work of art towards the
> whole are readjusted; and this is conformity between the old
> and the new.[9]

There is confidence and hope in that, as well as modesty, something both active and passive: Eliot may be able to bring
something to the tradition which will be good enough to alter
our view of it all: he will *identify* himself in relation to[10] the
whole as a young person shapes him- or herself *within* and *against*
the pre-existing circle of the family, who themselves change *in*
themselves and in their own relation *among* themselves as the
newcomer makes himself present. The relation between poet and
tradition is organic.

The part II variety of Impersonality attempts to explain how
the tradition in the form of a 'medium', affects the relation of the
poem to its author. The explanation, as it were, moves from outside Eliot to within him—but not upon the personality; upon the
'poetry and not the poet'. The emphasis upon 'poetry' is part of
a general stress on the *art-object* (it is a part of his criticism which
derives most obviously from French *aesthetic* thought): 'poetry',
in Mallarmé's rebuking formation, 'is not made from ideas, but
words'. This Impersonality thus connects with Eliot's other
'theory'—that of the 'objective correlative'. And in like fashion
the second-version 'emotions' are 'components' which are 'used',
are 'worked-up'; experience 'enters into combination' with other
matters. Such things are 'elements'—are treated 'objectively',
too. To them, the mind of the poet is a 'catalyst', producing a
concentration 'which does not happen consciously or of de-
liberation'.

This Impersonality has been described by C. K. Stead as 'an
escape further into the self' rather than an escape from the self; a

going-below the conscious 'personality' which is a superficial end-product of historical dissociation. It stands in Tradition as a sort of inner suspension (perhaps a reflection of 'negative capability') in contrast to the effort of 'acquiring' the impersonality of tradition. Both impersonalities seem to want to emphasize the 'art-object' but in different ways. The attempt *seems* to be to see tradition as an organic 'structure'; the poem likewise; the 'emotions', 'feelings' and 'experiences' are constituents of the poem in a wordless condition. When Eliot moves within 'the poet' he offers us the beginnings of a kind of general science of artistic creation. Words are the first 'objects' (language as a whole might be the next) in a chain of mediation which received expression in the last of our 'theories',[11] that of the 'objective correlative':

> The only way of expressing emotion in the form of art is by finding an 'objective correlative'; in other words, a set of objects, a situation, a chain of events which shall be the formula of that *particular* emotion; such that when the external facts, which must terminate in sensory experience, are given, the emotion is immediately evoked. If you examine any of Shakespeare's more successful tragedies, you will find this exact equivalence; you will find that the state of mind of Lady Macbeth walking in her sleep has been communicated to you by a skilful accumulation of imagined sensory impressions; the words of Macbeth on hearing of his wife's death strike us as if, given the *sequence* of events, these words were *automatically released* by the last *event* in the *series*.[12] (My italics.)

This perilously behaviourist language[13] is another example of Eliot's trying to 'see the object as it really is', in another register from that of 'pure contemplation' in 'that stage of vision *amor intellectualis Dei*' (see above, p. 4); another attempt in different terms to transcend the conditions of the self, and unify the dissociation of personality (for if 'personality' is the result of the dissociation of sensibility, then sensibility is a virtual synonym for personality).

It is in the continual passing associations of terms (such as 'object' with 'contemplation' above; or of 'contemplation of the object' with 'impersonality', with 'devotion' with 'facing facts' with 'the clear glass of vision' with—at last— 'innocence' in the uncollected essay on Macchiavelli)[14] that one catches, and loses, and catches again the preoccupation of the four 'theories'. We see them, see that they 'go together' and try to offer a sense of what Eliot 'really meant'—before they slip away again.

I have tried to give my explanation of the connections between utterances which revolve about the central attempt to achieve an Impersonality which will be a transcendence of a formless age and fulfilment as a poet. However, a number of things have to be said. First, such an exposition has to be reconstructed. Eliot never did it himself. And therefore we can *never be quite sure* that we are presenting him accurately. There is always the doubt which only he could have dispelled by saying what he meant himself. He might not approve of my paraphrase—and nor might many of his commentators. Secondly, the fact that he did not do it is itself of great importance—*what does it mean?* Is there not some kind of dissociation in itself, here? Of this kind?: 'He who reads this . . . will observe at once its fragmentary nature, but after some study will perceive the fragmentariness lies in the expression more than the thought.'[15] And to give the key a further turn: do we admit dissociation when we allow such a separation of thought and expression, content and form? Does the unified sensibility speak in that way? And following from that we must be prompted to ask why Eliot did not make a clear statement of his own implication in his own 'theory' of dissociation. Such an admission may be the final key to transcendence; or how do those who are dissociated escape the dissociation?

One might say briefly, that Eliot's concentration upon, contemplation-of, the object, corresponds to Arnold's wish to 'see life steadily and see it whole'. In both an impersonality is required. But they are bound to be different, *because the words in which they are expressed are different.* And if one can emulate Eliot and try and say something pregnant and brief of one's own it is this: that in the difference between the words 'life', 'steady' and 'whole' and Eliot's 'external facts', 'objective correlative' and 'impersonality' is registered another 'something that has happened to the mind of England'. Eliot expresses that something. For us, who come later still, the need and the difficulty is to see him whole. It is a matter of urgency.

CHAPTER I

Critical Responsibility and Critical Approach

THE ISSUE

The 'theory' of Impersonality as it appears in T. S. Eliot, Pound, Hulme and others I shall take to be still an issue, a living issue,[1] and one which we have not settled with ourselves. There is a temptation to say that the issue lives *even though* the word Impersonality makes us uneasy; it is so near in form and meaning to our commoner 'depersonalize' and 'depersonalization' with their discomfiting adjunct 'dehumanize'. But the uneasiness might as well be brought into the foreground as a reason why the issue lives. In our world, different of course from Eliot's of half a century or so ago but not so different that our dilemmas are fundamentally changed, the word *impersonality* touches the fear that our society has already aroused in us—that it may require us to be less than we are, less perhaps than we might be. When a student, the last vestige of the disappearing 'common reader', hears of the necessity in the creation of a lasting literature for 'the continual extinction of personality' he is unlikely not to wonder about the possible threat to his personality, his self, for which he may already feel that he has to fight. In teaching today this is a frequent, if not an invariable, reaction, often accompanied (I would like to testify) by expressions of repugnance and rejection which spread from the criticism—and particularly from 'Tradition and the Individual Talent'—to the poetry.

If we don't find these actions difficult to discuss, we can hardly be taking the issue seriously. They go deep, are frequently instinctive, and have their roots outside the bounds of literature as an 'objective' or semi-objective 'discipline' of explication and understanding (though, of course, most of the statements to which I shall refer will come from within the profession of criticism,

academic or other). We should consider, for a start, whether
the repugnance and rejection are proper. If so, these objections
cannot be met *from within* the historical-philosophical presupposi-
tions of literary theory. It will not do *just* to connect what Eliot
says with what Pound or Hulme say, with de Gourmont, Benda,
Aristotle, Aquinas, or Scholasticism.[2] The *reader's* question, arising
from the sense of his own circumstances, remains: and the normal
terms of the discussion of literary theory, must be extended to
meet it, although they may do well enough for answering other
questions. Nor will it do to revert from external to internal
explication—to refer to a web of connections within Eliot's own
criticism. For one thing, those connections are not always what
they seem, have many cunning passages and contrived corridors,
that explication can too readily try to make straight. For another,
and at the moment far more important thing, the abiding question
is precisely one of personality, understood as character and self,
unmediated by the devices of a professional competence. In reading Eliot's criticism a contest develops between self and self, the
reader's and Eliot's; and it is just this which makes the issue a
living one, the persisting importance of which can be testified to
by that deep desire to sweep aside—a force of rejection that is not
by any means only a symptom of new attitudes in new genera-
tions.[3] We find it in an article by the late James Smith,[4] even after
we have made the necessary discount for the Professor's sense of
'duty to sow discord' at an academic colloquium, when he says
that Eliot—whose own remark on Hobbes is being modified[5]—
was one of 'those extraordinary land-loupers whom the chaotic
motions of the early twentieth century tossed into an eminence
which they hardly deserved and which—at least yet—they have
never lost'. The force of that returns later when Smith refers to
the theory of impersonality in the 'notorious' 'Tradition and the
Individual Talent', which

> . . . withdraws the work of art so far from the stench and noise
> of any jungle as to be inhumanly free from either: as an instru-
> ment in an operating theatre, as unvocal as an image in a church.
> Produced, it would seem, by the fortuitous concourse of
> numberless feelings, phrases, images stored in the mind as a
> mere receptacle, the work of art bears no trace of a mind about

it, for that would prejudice its purity. Not without a feeling of justification, therefore,[6] Eliot adopts phrases from the Gospel: 'The Arts,' he intones, 'insist that a man shall dispose of all that he has . . . and follow art alone.' Certainly a man must dispose, that is, he must get rid of, what he usually values most highly: his personality, or his very self.

One's doubts about Professor Smith's tone—the too-obviously polemical metaphors, the affected high-handedness (high-table-ness?)—don't dispel the comprehensive force of the conclusion: it *is* what many people feel.[7] The recoil from 'Tradition and the Individual Talent' is not by any means entirely unjust: Eliot (as I shall hope to make plain in the next chapter) in many particular parts of that essay, *asks* for it. If one has not felt some repugnance, in fact, one can only have been reading the essay in a way that has made an insulation against it: as 'pure argument', or as 'pure theory', or perhaps in a scholarly way: in *any* way that, however 'useful', may advert one to only a part of what is there. That is not too difficult. And is even hard to say 'however' without introducing that too-bland judiciousness that merely glosses-over deeper issues . . . However . . . the strength of the recoil can do one thing we ought not to allow: withdraw us so far from Eliot in sympathy that we forget that here (and Eliot sometimes makes the reader feel that he would be happier if we did forget) there may be, if not a 'jungle' at least some kind of a human tangle; a set of paradoxes *of personality itself*. A good deal of Eliot's criticism by now lives for such reasons alone—in a curiously patchy, but at the same time forceful, manner.

SEPARATION AND RELATION

The tangle of paradoxes begins with Eliot's own separation of the poet from the man, 'the man who suffers from the mind which creates'. For the idea of impersonality requires an idea of per-sonality, just as an idea of 'good' requires one of 'bad', or an idea of 'inhumanity' needs one of 'humanity'. In order that there should be detachment there must be things from which the detachment is made. Eliot's 'theory' in 'Tradition and the Indivi-dual Talent', which offers (science-wise) a 'definition' of the

'process' of impersonalization, must entail a corresponding muta-
tion *within* the idea of personality. The paradox, as I hope we shall
come to understand, is that the virtue of impersonality rests upon
the aesthetic-moral dubiousness of the 'personality' from which
Eliot wishes to 'escape'; a dubiousness which is ensured, in this
essay but by no means always elsewhere, by Eliot's use of words
like 'escape'; which are in their turn subverted by saying (for
example) that 'only those who have personality and emotions
know what it means to want to escape from these things'.[8] It
sounds in the end—or does it?—as though these things *are* worth
having . . . and so we are introduced to a new uncertainty: are the
words *impersonality* and *personality* in a stable relation? If the idea,
or the 'theory', of Impersonality is to be clear enough, then the
idea of personality must be clear enough (but not necessarily
defined, as Eliot often offers to do: 'there remains to define this
process of depersonalization').[9] The sufficient clarity should be of
the same kind as we find in our ordinary uses of *good* and *bad*,
right and *wrong*: clear enough to be settled, but not so tightly
fixed as to prohibit the perpetual necessary modifications of terms,
of *moral* terms, that life and change and the living language in
which life and change are expressed require. The two terms should
hang together.

One thing, then, that Eliot's use of the word *impersonality* in
part II in particular of 'Tradition and the Individual Talent' should
make us do is ask how his use of the word *personality* corresponds.
Is it consistent in itself? Does it support and modify its sibling-
term? Chapter 3 is an attempt to answer such questions through
the examination of a considerable number of uses of *personality*
scattered throughout the whole of Eliot's criticism . . . But this
would still not be enough to temper the kind of rejection that is
still made of Eliot's criticism to a properly judicious understanding, not less sure, but more *ondoyant et divers*.

The real *issue*, in short, is one of relationship—the kind that
must obtain in any aesthetic-moral universe of terms. Eliot—it is
part of his very great importance—was aware with peculiar keen-
ness that the balance *between* the world and himself (to reduce all
such terms to a convenient pair) was dislocated, unhelpful to him
as a poet: 'in a formless age there is very little hope for the minor
poet'—a class of which he sometimes claimed himself a member.

As F. W. Bateson has remarked, introducing another relation: 'The crucial problem, as Eliot was almost the first to realize, was the nature of the relationship between the individual genius and the medium he employed.'[10] The particular importance of the pair Personality-Impersonality is that in Eliot's critical writing it is the focus of all the other relations: to put the matter into more obviously psychological-philosophical terms, it is a distillation to Self and Other. The urgent question for us—which inevitably gives the literary discussion a moral extension—is whether those relations are kept sufficiently stable within the criticism. Could they be? And if not, why? Perhaps, if the terms *were* settled, and therefore were clear, there would be less need for interpretation and for re-interpretation, for 'translating' of them out of one category into another, from the 'aesthetic' into the psychological, the psychological into the moral:

> Eliot's explanation that 'the poet has not a "personality" to express, but a particular medium, in which impressions and experiences combine in particular and unexpected ways' becomes immediately intelligible if it is translated out of psychology into aesthetics and if we substitute '*persona*' for 'medium'. A personality, however much 'a conduit of urgent life', will only tend to express itself; a *persona*, on the other hand, is essentially non-autobiographical, non-egocentric.[11]

But is 'medium' a psychological term? *Is* 'persona' a proper substitute? In what sense are Browning's or Pound's 'personae' non-egocentric? Is it inevitable that we *only* express ourselves when we express ourselves? Can't *personality* be used in ways which would include that which is not of ourselves alone? Are these substitutions-for and translations-between one vocabulary and another really going to help the establishment of settled common uses of such words in ordinary language? Couldn't the very existence of multiple vocabularies be one of the problems, the consequent shifting of the terms a symptom of the very insecurity Eliot was trying to counter? Asking so many questions may be enough on its own to make one feel insecure. You can as well argue over the meaning of this set of terms as that, in infinite extension—or regression. And the only guard against doing so is common-sense, the common-sense of common usage coming from common cultural assumptions; the assumptions which Eliot evidently felt the lack of, and we may well feel the lack of too. If we are not sure what we mean by *personality* (which would be *not* to have an instinctive feeling for its place in our full moral vocabulary), what does that in itself mean, for our *selves*?

PERSONALITY AND SELF

That is the question, that is the word, whose prompting lies behind the repugnance and accompanying rejection referred to before. Our selves are the issue, in their relation to other things—however specialist-literary, or aesthetic-philosophic the argument sometimes appears. An interest in the matter must be instinctive, for anyone: Eliot kept his under the guise of personality; but it was a deep preoccupation, reflected in his constant, if fragmentary, returns to it, and it is not consequently easy to square it with a wish to 'escape from' personality. Such a preoccupation need not be egotistical at all, but the reverse, a necessary part of identity. And it is an implicit part of the interpretation being offered here that Eliot's criticism should raise, for all of us, issues such as these:

'Self' is the dangerous element which links us yet threatens to make us anti-social. We have, now, other related words given to us by our culture: we ask tentatively whether we may safely distinguish between that self, the ego—the *moi* as the seventeenth-century French put it—and something more proper to us, the identity. The self, we are learning to say, is universal, closed, and in a bad sense, stable: the identity is open, therefore capable of growth, and individuating. It could be something to which one owes a duty, not incompatible (or not always) with social duty. A good society is composed of, or encourages, growing identities, which pursue their own development. It is clear that Racine had no such words available to him; clear also that he would dismiss the distinction as an unreal and dangerous delusion . . . it is important to keep him somewhere in view as a profound negative voice when we offer ourselves the possible comfort implicit in the distinction between self and identity.[12]

If the rejection of Eliot comes from a threatened sense of self or even of identity, any reply to it must be made from similar ground for there to be any hope of a critical meeting. Reactions from self can't be met by arguments from theory. We ourselves *must* speak personally. What, after all, is to be said of that *person* T. S. Eliot who himself said that the mind of the poet was a 'finely perfected medium'[13] which has 'only a medium and not a personality',[14] to express? A medium expressing a medium—can we really imagine being that?

But these are questions that we are inhibited from asking by Eliot himself. We should 'concentrate on the poetry and not on the poet'.[15] And indeed, we should try to avoid psychology, not chiefly because of incompetence in that field, or because of the impertinence that might be offered to Eliot, if we did not, or even because, challenged, we wish to meet Eliot on his own ground; but because of the need to adhere to non-specialist language, the language of which literature is made and in which its criticism is still largely written.[16] To stick to such language is a necessary part of the delicacy that alone can justify overriding Eliot's distinction to ask—is it a proper distinction to make, or is it made, *here*, with a motive? The questions we are asking are themselves, after all, simple and inevitable and don't come from any specialist part of ourselves. Why did Eliot *need* a 'theory' of Impersonality (he wasn't alone, of course)? No doubt the inner need reflected an outer pressure—very well then, what was the relation between them, and can that relation be expressed in ways that don't infringe the proper privacies of personality? In a fair number of asides—he found them significantly congenial—Eliot expressed his sense of the unfriendliness of the world towards the poet, reflected in the development of English literary history:

> What I see, in the history of English poetry, is not so much daemonic possession [Eliot is here answering some 'romantic' views of Sir Herbert Read's] as the splitting-up of personality ... Nor can you isolate poetry from everything else in the history of a people.[17]

Nor can you for long dissociate a literary 'theory' from what surrounds it—from the need for it, the needs that reflect the pressure, the reciprocation of inner and outer—the ecology, as it were, of the theory-plant. The element of the man, as Eliot recognizes, is his time; but he may not be, as the common phrase implies, happily at home 'in' it. And Eliot, in his prominence, is the focus —the 'point of intersection'—for an interest that cannot be contained within the explication of theory as a subsidiary part-of-a-part of Literary Criticism. If we alter the proper name, and somewhat reduce our expectations, the following is to the point:

> The life of Rilke must be entered: its fundamental problems springing from his times, its . . . human struggle and its possibility of release rooted deeply in its own being. He who has made this entry (*intellectual interest is not enough*) . . . will be amazed by the simplicity of the experience.[18] (My italics.)

INNOCENCE AND EXEGESIS

One would be more confident of the virtue of 'intellectual interest', of literary explication, if Eliot's criticism were agreed to be more coherent than it is—coherent in the 'classical' way of which we can take Aristotle's *Poetics*, Johnson's various writings, or—even—Coleridge's *Biographia Literaria* as coherent: behind each lies a confident set of assumptions, or a *sufficiently* clear animating principle (whether they are agreeable to us is not the present point) giving just that consistency to the whole that Eliot's criticism lacks, that *lacunae* of logic, conventionalities or blunders of judgment don't *essentially* damage. But Eliot's essays are mainly consistent in their inconsistencies; their fluctuations between fineness and banality, their insecurities of tone, their internal contradictions (sometimes between sentence and sentence), their pseudo-arguments balancing a quite unique incisiveness of insight. Some of these things have been remarked on often enough:

> Eliot is a theorist who has repeatedly contradicted himself on every important issue that he has touched. Between some of his contradictory statements there is a greater or less lapse of time, and one might account for them by a change of view if he showed any consistency of contradiction; but many of them occur within the same book or even within the same essay.[19]

Winters is Eliot's most intransigeant critic—but there is a certain innocence in his rebuke—the innocence of one who knows what the standards (of theory) are, but whose knowledge is a prophylactic against another kind of understanding. It is the innocence of a certain sort of confidence and stability: the boy has not come up to scratch—the boy must go back to his desk. The difficulty, of course, as in all pedagogy, is to maintain the line and at the same time bend from it—perhaps an impossibility. Again: 'There is in Eliot's writings an immediate critical sense which is expert and infallible, but it consists with theoretical innocence. Behind it is no great philosophical habit, nor philosophical will, to push through it to definition.'[20] There is an innocence in this, too, different but connected. It is that of the theorists—an innocence that stops Crowe Ransom from finding it odd that Eliot, with his philosophical training at Harvard, his thesis on Bradley, should be wanting in these things. What does *that* mean?—the questions cannot really even be asked by those who want to keep the argument to the line of 'theory' and 'philosophy'. Eliot has done his philosophy, and it hasn't seemed to help. Could it? Is it what *we* need?[21]

> And again:

> this distinction seems to be an important one; but how he intends it to be taken cannot be gathered from the content . . . this statement can hardly be taken as a mere slip on Eliot's part, and yet it is hard to believe that he actually means what he says . . . Seemingly he is not aware of the difficulties which the shift brings with it . . . whether Eliot means one or the other alternative is not clear . . . these statements stock a bewildering puzzle . . . It should now be clear that Eliot hesitates between two propositions.[22]

And finally: 'It is an interesting passage. One could use it to argue . . . and one could argue the opposite . . .'[23] No more affidavits are necessary just here. These things are being said about the man who is acknowledged to be the founder of our criticism; a great literary critic, a man who altered and rejuvenated the tradition of criticism as he did that of verse. There is no need to question that judgment too deeply at present, but we do have to ask how it is that the acknowledged classic status can co-exist with such verdicts. What kind of greatness can it be? What, fundamentally, does it spring from?—not, obviously, from the same source as more theoretical or professional criticism. A great critic who cannot think consistently—it does seem to be a puzzle to which the conventional answer, that Eliot's was the criticism of a poet, comes nowadays far too pat. It is like a new way of saying that poets are naturally self-contradictory and inconsistent—wayward creatures: they should be sent away from the Republic. The up-to-date conventionality may even mask a sentimentally-romantic view of the poet—preferably *maudit*—as well as the possibility of a superiority: the other kind of criticism can correct the natural vagaries—with *theory*, with *philosophy*. Moreover, the judgement accepts a division between two different kinds of criticism, which echoes and accepts a principle of division within Eliot's own (between poet and man, between critic and poet, between theory and life) which should be taken as a clue to understanding but not acceded-to. Wordsworth saw the poet as essentially the same as other men:

> The poet writes under one restriction only, namely, the necessity of giving immediate pleasure to a human being possessed of that information which may be expected of him, not as a lawyer, a mariner, an astronomer, or a natural philosopher, but as a man.[24]

Eliot sees him as different:

> When a poet's mind is perfectly equipped for its work, it is constantly amalgamating disparate experience; the ordinary man's experience is chaotic, irregular, fragmentary.[25]

What is entailed in the change of a century?

If Eliot's criticism is taken as that of a poet as opposed to another category of being, contemporary criticism hardly accepts one possible consequence of this judgment: that its own distinction assists a division. It is open to us, after all, to read the essays as just that: as *expression*, not as theory; as one might read literature, continuous with poetry—with Eliot's own poetry. But on the contrary, they are generally read (Vincent Buckley's book is one near exception) as if they were rational *statement*. It is thus (though paradoxically) that the dividedness of the approach helps us to maintain the two central essays, 'Tradition and the Individual Talent' (1919) and 'The Function of Criticism' (1923) as classics at the same time as we discover them to be full of inconsistencies. And of course, reading it in what has become the more usual way —*the other way* of commentary and explication—is useful, offering as it does to make what might be felt to be difficult or obscure plainer, to show the connections between the preoccupations of the criticism and the poetry that goes with it, setting both in their literary or 'aesthetic' context: here is T. S. Eliot among the Last Romantics, or in opposition to the Georgians, with this intellectual inheritance from America (Hawthorne, Henry Adams, Henry James), that from France (*symbolisme*, de Gourmont, Laforgue, Valéry . . .) and so on.

Eliot's essays are—in a particular sort of way—concentrated to the point of ellipsis, and do need some teasing-out. The exegeticists talk *about* the same things that Eliot feels a pressure on himself to speak of (a pressure or need which the concentration may be thought to express—perhaps involuntarily)—that knot of 'problems' that tightens in Eliot's discussion of them around the relations of the poet to his world, his present to its present and past, the new to the traditional, of personality to established order, inner psychology to outer society: the very nexus of them is the idea of Impersonality. But often out of the good intention of making the best case of an admired subject, the explications tend to an explaining-away. The purpose being to make sense *of*, sense (good or not so good) is made: a straight piece of string—useful! —is drawn out of all those tangles and knots. One critic, at least, has remarked in an aside that, 'Those early ideas of Eliot's . . . have [been] tidied-up and made more systematic than he intended them to be . . .'[26]

A warrant for this, as well as for a more general criticism-of-the-criticism, can be found in passing remarks of Eliot's own. Can a man who declares himself thus, be viewed as a 'theoretician'? There is surely something else here, *to be read*:

The point of view I am struggling to attack is perhaps related to the metaphysical theory of the substantial unity of the soul: for my meaning is that the poet has not a 'personality' to express, but a particular medium . . .[27]

By way of helping writer and reader with the struggle, explanatory criticism will take the word 'medium' or 'personality' and
try to say what is meant by them, making connections perhaps
with other 'key words', the other bits of Eliot's 'theory' of poetic
creativity. To do that is to use one's attentiveness selectively, to
notice (maybe with a sort of cultural conformity) one thing before
another thing. But there *are* other things to notice—which an
interest in literary *ideas* might well regard as trivial. *This* kind of
thing (although the particular example is useful largely because it
sees the opposite of what I do): 'What strikes one particularly
about them [the critical essays] is their strongly rhetorical manner.
The tone is immediately authoritative and magisterial, and there
is a *gravitas* of syntax and phrasing, a studied 'placing' of writers
that often recalls Johnson.'[28] While it is right to take note of these
matters, a more general, or ordinary, attention will frequently
tell us something else about Eliot in his essays, and present in the
quotation above. How can you be authoritative or magisterial if
you declare that you are struggling (would Dr Johnson ever have
said that he was—like that?); and what is the phrase about the
theory of the soul doing there? (Eliot doesn't explain it, he just
says it and jumps forward)—except to get over an insecure patch
by cowing the reader with a bit of learned swagger? The un-
theoretical reader might want an answer to these questions first,
and above all. Why so, really, *un*magisterial and *un*authoritative?
Because he did not notice it; then why didn't he notice it—
because he was careless, because he couldn't? To bring such
general attention to what Eliot says as *expression*, rather than as
theory, is to see something different from the usual that—if we
see enough of it—may tell us something new about 'Tradition
and the Individual Talent'.

Moreover, Eliot the critic, the rational conscious 'personality'
(to use the word as Eliot often does) is writing here about a matter
of the first importance to Eliot the poet, or even the person. To
ask 'why does he write like this about this' is to try to talk about
the theory *in its place*, undetached from the expression of it. That
is the meaning of 'context' here. Although it is almost standard
practice to deal with Eliot's essays by saying that it is the criticism
of a poet (Eliot of course dealt with himself in this way:

... a by-product of my private poetry-workshop; or a pro-
longation of the thinking that went into the formation of my
own verse ...');[29]

although, thus, the particular reference is emphasized at the ex-
pense of the possible general truth, we still proceed with our
outlining and connection-tracing; extracting and extending a
framework about and away from the texts, which should implicitly
include the poetry itself. But, because it is criticism, it is not any
less a 'text'. Moreover, to 'demonstrate' that this or that is what
was meant is not-to-do the very thing that our initial judgment
imposes: it is *not to* attend to the criticism primarily *as* that of a
poet. To do the reverse—to attend to it in *that* way—you must
surely treat the criticism in the same way as you treat a poem;
and if we do that we may agree that 'Tradition and the Individual
Talent' is much nearer to the condition of poetry, and particularly
Eliot's own, than it is to that of exegetical criticism which is more
likely to aspire to the nature of philosophy. Even so:

> In most of the histories of philosophy that I know, philosophic
> systems are presented to us as if growing out of one another
> spontaneously, and their authors, the philosophers, appear only
> as mere pretexts. The inner biography of the philosophers ...
> occupies a secondary place. And yet it is precisely this inner
> biography that explains for us most things.
>   It behoves us to say, before all, that philosophy lies closer to
> poetry than science ... the sciences are in a certain sense more
> foreign to us than philosophy ... our philosophy—that is, our
> mode of understanding or not understanding the world and
> life springs from our feeling towards life itself. And life, like
> everything affective, has roots in subconsciousness, perhaps
> even in the unconscious.[30]

And criticism *must* lie closer to poetry than philosophy, further
away from science. If exegetical or academic criticism looks in the
other direction, it must move away from the essays: there must be
matters that its habits cannot explain. One method, as one habit,
makes other methods difficult, or impossible: not only that, it
makes the truly *general* harder to attain. It is thus that explicatory
criticism can find itself saying:

It may be objected that Eliot has written things which seem to contradict what I have said . . . My answer to this is, first, that I am not responsible for Eliot's self-contradictions; second, that where there are contradictions, I have concentrated on those remarks which seem most honestly to proceed from Eliot's experience as an artist . . .[31]

The slight irritation here is revealing. Of *course* he's not responsible for them: only Eliot could be. But where does Stead see his own responsibility as ending? The contradictions are still there, in turn contradicting what Stead says Eliot meant: and the critic whose approach won't accommodate them turns his back. Stead really sees his responsibility as ending with his 'approach'.

We find the same underlying reaction in others. Although only three, I hope telling, examples of it are quoted here, it is much more widespread than that—and not, incidentally, restricted to Eliot-criticism. The reaction is continuous with the demand for theoretical consistency noted earlier in Winters, Ransom and Vivas. Of course, from the point of view of theory, it is a perfectly proper demand and would be a sufficient one if that point of view were the only one, if it were a sort of *Weltanschauung*. But theories can't be that, and further, cannot really make sense of Eliot's criticism because it isn't, *precisely*, what it proposes itself as, a *theory*—despite Eliot's own liberal play with that very word. Literary theory cannot accommodate Eliot's carelessness, even his carelessness about his contradictions—its practitioners have to say that it doesn't count—it doesn't *really mean* anything. So they end up in the position of Stead above, or even of Buckley in his careful, sensitive, patient, fair book: 'See also the astonishing and untypical judgment about Ben Jonson's work . . . I do not want to analyze this judgment in detail because it is untypical.'[32] But it is typical of Eliot to make 'untypical' judgments. It is precisely this essay which Stead uses to show the real underlying coherence of Eliot's terms, which 'recur in varying contexts, but are set consistently in opposition to one another'[33]—the opposition being of two basic categories, the impersonal and the personal. But even here there are difficulties, if we agree that the personal includes the impersonal.[34] Can a conception that includes another conception stand in opposition to it, without a distortion of our normal language-use? And with such a distortion of the normal how sure can we feel of what is typical and what isn't? The truth is that Eliot does not lend himself in his criticism to measurement by straight-edge. In fact, it has to be said (and will be later) that his reasoning is very frequently a mere appearance of reason. And so we find it repeatedly, and rather touchingly and plaintively said: 'Is there a contradiction of the statements on the autonomy of poetry exemplified above? Or what does Eliot really mean?'[35] This is, surely, the innocence of the rational man. Thought of in one way, what Eliot means is everything that Eliot says, leaving nothing out, reading him fully, through and through. But this is not how Smidt wishes to use the phrase: our ordinary use is present ('there's something behind all this'—which is much more the sense of it that I wish to pursue) but only superficially, for Smidt really wants a consistent Eliot purified of muddle. The 'really' tells us so.

The trouble with the sense-finding, consistency-claiming approaches of the explicatory critics is that it leads them into a sort of logical enclosure,[36] rather more of an impasse than a passing nuisance. Based on the passage above it would go in this way: Eliot did not say what he really meant; so what he really meant was something he did *not* say: what Eliot really meant becomes something that *we* say. This can only happen if we want Eliot to mean something in particular, a certain sort of thing; if we bring our motives (the motives, ironically enough, of reason and 'detachment') to Eliot, and don't simply read him, fully, contradictions and all.

READING THE REMAINS

A Winters or a Vivas, who wish to say simply that the criticism is an incorrigible muddle, and a Stead or a Smidt, who want to discover 'what Eliot really meant' co-exist within the same set of assumptions. The first cannot explain the extraordinary hold that Eliot's criticism still has, testified to not merely by the presence of 'Tradition and the Individual Talent' in standard 'readers' in criticism, but also by statements such as those of F. R. Leavis, describing the impression made upon him by his first purchase of *The Sacred Wood*.[37] Eliot's essays grip as theory never grips. Exegetical criticism cannot explain it, with its placid assumption that the *whole* of what Eliot said can be overlooked, that it is proper to disconnect or separate a part from the whole to make sense. But what are we to make of what is left behind? It is really so 'trivial'?:

> To see how the consistent self-depreciation masks but also reveals a sustained attack that Eliot made upon himself, we should perhaps divert our attention from its central manifestations and the way in which it conditions Eliot's achievement as a whole, and concentrate rather upon the trivial or peripheral ways in which it betrays itself. In this connection a study of Eliot's inconsistencies, of the way, we might say, in which he was compelled to deny an idea of his own once he had asserted it, might be very revealing as to his general temperament.[38]

The paradoxical nature of what we find if we read Eliot's criticism openly, without any however well-intentioned wish to 'make sense of' his 'theories' is recognized here by Wollheim (the remark is particularly notable coming from a philosopher) in 'masks but also reveals'. And to encounter paradox is somewhat unnerving: things should preferably be clear, being unconfused by seeming—confusion confuses us. Read openly, but minutely, inconsistency is found to be in every part of his essays, not just 'in the argument', and the fluctuations are present throughout his career as a critic, in the early work that is still much admired and in the later criticism that is so little. In this—to be paradoxical oneself—they are consistent, although over the years the consistencies (for example, the first part of 'Tradition and the Individual Talent', the essays on Marvell and Massinger) and the inconsistencies shift and change in nature: the later consistency is too often one of conventionality.[39]

Something more than well-justified complaints that things don't hold water seems to be needed. Why do these things happen? What explanation can be found for the contradictions? Is there a deeper, if inverted, consistency to be found, and might it have anything to do with the doctrine of Impersonality and that in turn with the scattered remarks that Eliot makes about Personality: and why is Eliot, Eliot particularly but not Eliot alone, interested in these things? Have those other 'theories'—on the dissociation of sensibility and the objective correlative, mere beginnings of theories lasting only a paragraph or so and then left—have they some subterranean connection with personality? One can say, without uncalled-for infringement of the privacy of the poet-critic, that Eliot's references to the issue of personality continually emerge even from the conventional surface of much of the later criticism with the force and illumination of a personal concern—and then, as so often, are turned away from—as though he has recognised someone he cannot bring himself to meet:

> For the development of genuine taste, founded on genuine feeling, is inextricable from the development of personality and character. Genuine taste is always imperfect taste—but we are all, as a matter of fact, imperfect people; and the man whose taste in poetry does not bear the stamp of his particular personality . . . is apt to be a very uninteresting person with whom to discuss poetry.

followed by this odd nervous-sounding footnote:

> In making this statement, I refuse to be drawn into any discussion of the definition of 'personality' and 'character'.[40]

The question here is not so much Why not? as Why add this footnote at all? He has just said what he thinks; it is perfectly plain; the words are used as we all use them. But he cannot rest on his own statement: the footnote makes it seem that what he has said he has blurted-out and would half-like to withdraw—but no, he won't—and that then sounds like an obstinacy. He has revealed himself, wants to mask himself—but finally must reveal: an insecurity or instability. One can't help but feel that this has happened because he has said something *personal*. And is there not an instability also in the footnote? '*The* definition'—his definition? a general 'scientific' definition? a single definition rather than definitions? His use of the phrase doesn't settle clearly to any one of these: it wants, itself, the definition of a confident use. We cannot rest too much on this of course, but the possibility does present itself that the pressure of an interest can come precisely from an insecurity about the very subject of interest.

The inconsistency-instability here is a very minor example, and at present it is more important to emphasize the personal directness of the statement, its emphasis on the personal. How might the stress on the personal nature of taste in poetry fit with the equally forcefully put demand for 'the continual extinction of personality' in the poet? It is not enough to say of course that the word is being differently used: why does Eliot want to use the same word, and not a synonym? The different uses reflect a fundamental disjunction in the poet. His own taste is not continuous between his reading and his writing. In ordinary language there is a plain enough relation between *personality* and *impersonality*; but in Eliot's use in his criticism as a whole the relation is shifting and disinclined to resolve itself, as we shall see. (A further reflection of this is Eliot's own ambiguous relation to 'Tradition and the Individual Talent', his half-repudiations and half-justifications of it.) And something must be said of these shifts, contradictions and inconsistencies: they mean something, a meaning we ignore if we say that he 'really meant' something else.

CRITICISM AND EXPRESSION

To ask these questions entails—though it is easy to wish that one could avoid the consequence—making criticism more personal, as regards ourselves and the object of our criticism. The inconsistencies within Eliot's criticism cannot lie anywhere but within the personality of Eliot himself (where else *could* one place them?). A more 'detached' or 'objective' 'approach' (to use the key words of contemporary criticism) would be unlikely to lead us close enough to the source of the confusions: on the other hand to wish merely to retain one's hold on good sense is a different matter— but sense and detachment are not the same thing.

Eliot's essays, then, must simply be read, and read, largely but not quite entirely, as *expression*. By attending to the essays first in this way we try to refuse splitting something off, or acquiescing in a verbal separation into specialized personality-parts: critic/poet/man. Expression is of the man and to discuss it will, one hopes, help to close the gap between commentary and actuality— a little. This gap is the difference between criticism as it is largely practised today and the literature that is criticised. Our root assumption is that if we are to see that literature clearly we need to practise a proper detachment, on something like the lines of scientific objectivity. When we meet a criticism, like Eliot's, whose nature is different, we are uncertain how to deal with it: it is classed as 'a poet's criticism' without our seeing—because it is criticism—that we must then treat it at least in part as if it were literature. Our method puts blinkers on us: any method that is at all specialized does; it is the penalty that has to be paid, though we try to ignore the drain on our resources.

The gap between Eliot's poetry and his criticism is—despite Eliot's own occasional remarks—very narrow (a comparable case would be Eliot's own admired Valéry). It is much wider in Arnold —there is the opposing self of the prose, standing so strongly against the life of his times, and the more emollient self of the verse with its burdened sense of the 'iron times' of 'doubts, disputes, distractions, fears'. Eliot's public self, that of the Anglican social critic, is a more tentative construction than Arnold's, going with his acute sense of social division transferred into himself in a way that Arnold could never have done. Eliot accepts inner division, and makes it a part of his critical 'apparatus':

> that part of the poet's mind which rationalizes, constructs, and, in the rhetorician, illegitimately persuades and pleases at the expense of complex truth; and, on the other hand, that passive part of the mind which, independent of the will, negatively comprehends complexity, and provides images to embody it, but fails on its own to construct, assert, or even affirm.[41]

So Stead formulates the central opposition that inheres in Eliot's own use of words like 'feeling' as against 'emotion', 'image' against 'structure' and, above all, 'impersonal' against 'personal'. The question is whether, granted that Eliot's criticism was, as Stead remarks again, 'designed to bring into balance the two halves of the divided sensibility',[42] any kind of balance or of wholeness is achieved and, more important still, maintained, in the critical essays—the only proof of the success of the critical endeavour would be the sustained coherence of thought which is style. If Eliot accepts division as his starting point, can the terms of his subsequent discussion allow him to do much more than perpetuate, while illuminating, the division?[43] Is it likely that the balance will be anything more than temporary (say, as in a poem, where the temporary achievement can become permanent), embodied in style and image, qualities which are readily recognised as such powerful constituents of the essays even when the content is questionable and which constrain one to approach them—in Stead's terms they come from the 'passive' part of the mind—as one does a poem? Would not a truly subsisting wholeness incorporate the argument also, and 'theory' disappear into the complete texture?

It may be possible to show in the following chapters that the passive part of the mind distinguished by Stead is not separate in 'Tradition and the Individual Talent', that the reasoning and rationalizing Eliot-mind there shows a conceptual passivity which bears an organic relation to the ethos of his impersonality. But also, though not separated—as the parts of a machine can be thought of as separate—the elements are not at one, not psychologically united: they co-exist, and there is a continual switching between the two. A terminologically-established and sustained division is *in* the essay. Eliot half-knows it, and his subsequent critics can see some of it, but in the business of naming, separating and reasoning-out the existence of these divisions within a temperament that is not a whole, division is perpetuated, not healed. A 'dissociation of sensibility', if you like, is unconsciously acceded-to by much of the useful explicatory criticism which wishes to detach the ideas and argument from the very need which is revealed in the expression. If there is confusion, the confusion has a cause, but the 'impersonality' of analysis, the scientific affiliations of that particular variety of detachment, cannot help but take one away in spirit from Eliot's *personal* confusions. This 'rather confused piece of writing' (Stead), with its 'unintelligible' concept of impersonality (Winters) has had the kind of influence that rarely occurs with criticism, and that can come only from its expressive force, if its 'theories' are acknowledged as so dubious. It can't just be accounted-for by the opportunities it gives for explaining: it has a *more* than 'historical interest'. There is something in it that —perhaps one speaks for oneself—fascinates; a something reminiscent of Eliot's own comment on *Hamlet* (is it too soon to impute a discharge into semi-recognition, via the lightning-rod of another, of his own half-consciousness of his own condition?) It is puzzling and 'disquieting', there seems to be in it some 'superfluous and inconsistent' matter, 'workmanship and thought' are in 'an unstable condition', 'full of some stuff that the writer could not drag to light . . .'[44] The arresting force of these phrases is characteristic of Eliot's criticism, description and expression at once.

THE 'IMPERSONALITY' OF METHOD

All natural language is open to a *full* reading for a significance beyond what it is necessarily openly declaring—style and matter are one. Eliot's essays are no exception, though they aren't generally read in that way. There is no difficulty in our assenting to that proposition when it comes to letters, novels, poems, but we are slower to read philosophy, or science thus; or, for that matter, our own professional academic criticism. If Eliot accedes to a division, so does the practice of such a reading. How many academic critics reflect the literature they write about in the way that they write, one might ask abruptly, and what does it mean that they do not? One does not expect that critics of Lawrence should write like Lawrence—but that one self should present itself to another self in a style whose professional dedication consists in being recognizable, *personal* (there is no other word for it). There is no escaping the meanings of our chosen style; the signs can be read however 'objective' the writer wishes to be, however much he wishes to disappear into his communication. Scholarly style is, of course (and ironically), in part an attempt to do just that, and so achieve a version of Impersonality itself in detachment, in an 'objective judgment', of which we vainly hope no questions can be asked. Obedient to a method, we can free ourselves from responsibility and even perhaps error.[45] But not even scientific method can do this for us. And there is a penalty to pay if the style becomes an insulation. The case of 'Tradition and the Individual Talent' shows how an essay whose subject is a desired *impersonality* but which turns out to be (everyone agrees) very personal and to that extent *un*-theoretical, can be reconstructed into theoretic reasonableness through the set intentions of the academic critic. *Thus* the paradoxes develop.

So, even out of the self-imposed limitations of the style of objective criticism meanings can be read: *human* motives. What end has this limitation in view? As Wittgenstein wrote to Paul Engelmann: 'I am working reasonably hard and wish I were a better man and had a better mind. These two things are really one and the same.'[46] The attention and intelligence we bring to a piece of language, as to a person, need to be no more, simply, to have something to say, than the undifferentiated mind of one self. (And to say that at once raises the question of why it should be thought that to specialize is to make yourself *more*.) To be sure, some matters require more attention than others, but there is always something in a communication in natural language which is open to a general readiness of attention to see what is there to be seen in the whole as a whole. Only by a full reading can we escape the paradoxes of limitation. To say this is to lead back again to the remark that 'Tradition and the Individual Talent' asks us, if we are to explain it fully, to read it with the same general attention that we give to a poem, not as 'exposition' from which we might extract the 'ideas'.

CHAPTER II

Impersonality: 'Sacrifice' or 'Extinction'?

Sticking closely to the text of 'Tradition and the Individual Talent' is one way of *not* turning Eliot into a 'case'[1] for individual or social psychology, but still of being able to point, from the words of the text, towards if not at a division lying in origin beyond them. Eliot himself, of course, was conscious in a special way of the difficulties that face criticism in such matters; essentially those of all good manners and tact, not *peculiar* to the literary discipline. By simply reading his essay, one may bring the essential dividedness to light from within it and at the same time satisfy our own version of the standard that 'honest criticism and sensitive appreciation is directed not upon the poet but the poetry'. 'Exactly in what directions, and how far and in what terms should [one] force the answer?', as Geoffrey Grigson has asked: but there is no exactness to be stated, and no terms can be prescribed.[2] We can only see that things have been achieved or have not, and try and say why—though we can begin with the statement that, provoked by the full context and with the consequent more complete sense of motive, we may need to return to Eliot's own dictum with reservations to make. If we do direct our attention to sentence and paragraph we shall find division in places where it is not normally noted in any detail, in the very properties of manner: structure, grammar, and semantics. And this division first shows in a sudden distinct change in 'style' occurring *precisely at the point* where the essay itself divides into its two main sections: the first dealing with the 'outer' context of Tradition, the second turning to the 'inner' perspective of Impersonality. (The third section—a mere paragraph—is a concluding gesture where Eliot suggests that his essay offers 'practical conclusions [that] can be applied by the responsible person interested in poetry'.)

To be convincing about this change and its significance, very lengthy quotations will be needed, and still longer analyses, encompassing both grammar and (as it is called in Stylistics) *lexis*: the terms Eliot uses, what 'semantic field' they come from and how in his use of them, in their context, they are changed from other uses of them. Eliot, in section II, proposes a 'theory' of Impersonality which, if it had a substantial likeness to a scientific theory, would depend on a use of *terms* sufficiently similar to scientific use—that use which Sprat described as 'positive expressions, clear senses, bringing all things as near the Mathematical plainness, as they can'.[3]

I

The sections I have chosen for contrast come from pages 14 and 15 of section I, and pages 17–19 of II in *Selected Essays*. A second purpose of the examination (a purpose that could not be said to be actually subsidiary) will be to show just how *un*-Johnsonian Eliot's best manner actually is:

> Yet if the only form of tradition, of handing down, consisted in following the ways of the immediate generation before us in a blind or timid adherence to its successes, 'tradition' should positively be discouraged. We have seen many such simple currents soon lost in the sand; and novelty is better than repetition. Tradition is a matter of much wider significance. It cannot be inherited, and if you want it you must obtain it by great labour. It involves, in the first place, the historical sense, which we may call nearly indispensable to anyone who would continue to be a poet beyond his twenty-fifth year; and the historical sense involves a perception, not only of the pastness of the past, but of its presence; the historical sense compels a man to write not merely with his own generation in his bones, but with a feeling that the whole of the literature of Europe from Homer and within it the whole of the literature of his own country has a simultaneous existence and composes a simultaneous order. This historical sense, which is a sense of the timeless as well as of the temporal and of the timeless and of the temporal together, is what makes a writer traditional. And it is at the same time what makes a writer most acutely conscious of his place in time, of his own contemporaneity.

No poet, no artist of any art, has his complete meaning alone. His significance, his appreciation is the appreciation of his relation to the dead poets and artists. You cannot value him alone; you must set him, for contrast and comparison, among the dead. I mean this as a principle of aesthetic, not merely historical, criticism. The necessity that he shall conform, that he shall cohere, is not onesided; what happens when a new work of art is created is something that happens simultaneously to all the works of art which preceded it. The existing monuments form an ideal order among themselves, which is modified by the introduction of the new (the really new) work of art among them. The existing order is complete before the new work arrives; for order to persist after the supervention of novelty, the *whole* existing order must be, if ever so slightly, altered; and so the relations, proportions, values of each work of art toward the whole are readjusted; and this is conformity between the old and the new. Whoever has approved this idea of order, of the form of European, of English literature will not find it preposterous that the past should be altered by the present as much as the present is directed by the past. And the poet who is aware of this will be aware of great difficulties and responsibilities.

These two paragraphs have probably had as much critical influence as the theory of Impersonality *per se*, or of the remarks on the Objective Correlative, or the Dissociation of Sensibility, and have been the cause of a great deal less critical explanation. It is very rarely that they have seemed to offer themselves for the kind of dismissal given them by George Watson in *The Literary Critics*:

> . . . it is an odd historical sense that denies chronology, and conceives of the past both as 'the timeless and the temporal'; it might have been franker, one begins to feel as the essay proceeds, to call it the 'anti-historical' sense. It is a tribute to the fading power of historical studies that Eliot, like Arnold, seeks to maintain a facade of historicism . . . Contempt for historical criticism is confirmed in Eliot's argument as it develops . . .[4]

The more general feeling is that these words have a classic status, represented in part by its inclusion in readers of criticism, and also by the words of Frank Kermode: 'A new history of poetry was required, and Eliot sketched it: later it was filled out by others . . . The radical diagnosis is really to be found in a few pages of his critical essays.'[5] It is the part of the essay with which Leavis has not quarrelled: 'the idea of Tradition so incisively and provocatively formulated by him plays, I think, an essential part of the thinking of everyone today who is seriously interested in literature.'[6] If this is Eliot at his best as a critic, it will be well to start with these paragraphs to serve as a measure of excellence within an *oeuvre* which is so variable: it is not just a matter of the earlier as opposed to the later or even of the late, of there being a consistent falling-off, for there are extreme fluctuations in quality *throughout* Eliot's career as a critic. It is much more a case, as I hope I shall be able to show, of *this* Eliot here, in this essay, in this paragraph or even sentence, and *that* Eliot there, in another essay, or paragraph, or sentence. To demonstrate the particular quality of the excellence an analysis of some linguistic completeness is needed to stand to some extent against the subsequent even more detailed treatment of the second part of the essay. The individuality of the achievement of these paragraphs can be taken for brevity to be represented by a single sentence, that in the first paragraph beginning, 'It involves, in the first place . . .'

It is a long sentence—110 words or so—and if we give its construction the attention it deserves, we see that it revolves about the repetition of two key word-phrases, 'involves' and 'the/this historical sense'. It is *tradition* that involves the historical sense—but, by plain implication, it is not the only thing that it involves. That word is then transferred in the unwinding of the sentence, to the historical sense itself; as it were 'on the other side' of the mandarin (and condescending) clause directed at the young poet (a mild example of Eliot's fluctuating tone, where something objectionable just gets away from him). In this way the word 'involves' takes on a weight of meaning far exceeding our present inert use of it ('deeply involved in'): A is seen to contain B, among other things; and B in turn to contain C, also among other things. So the word, and with it the thought, moves towards *involution*. A sense of complexity is created, but free from a sense of the overburdeningly complicated. The word then does not re-occur, the rest of the structural weight being placed (as the sentence hovers on the verge of a more obvious rhetoric) on the phrase 'the historical sense'. In this initial section of the sentence, too, something else deserves notice—that the confidence of the syntax is modified by other 'stylistic items', particularly the use of the verb-forms known nowadays as the modal auxiliary, here *would* and *may*. Dubiety and confidence, tentativeness and rhetoric are combined.

Our preliminary sense of one-thing-included-in-another is increased by the 'failure' of the expectation of 'in the first place': there is no rhetorically-compensating second place, either verbally or conceptually: the 'and' preceding the second presentation of the phrase leads only to 'a perception' contained-in 'the sense'. The tendency towards a balancing is given a passing strengthening through the 'not only . . . but also' and 'not merely . . but with' collocations that follow. However, in the second case the surface parallelism gives onto a characteristic development: the 'but' presents us not with an equivalent conception to 'own generation in his bones' (which is the normal expectation of the device) but a complex of clauses echoing in their grammatical form the previously-judged involution. Abstraction ('the historical sense', 'generation') takes on a peculiar force through the verb *compels* and the colloquialism 'in his bones'—and these in turn discharge themselves into a 'feeling', again of one thing within another thing:

> the *whole* of the literature of Europe
> *and within it*
> the whole of the literature of his own country
> *has*
> a simultaneous existence
> *and composes*
> a simultaneous order.

All of this is a *feeling*, perception, or sense—it is an extraordinary expression of the charging of the individual sensibility with cultural responsibility and awareness. It is the *expression* that forces one to ask whether such an awareness was ever before required, let alone acknowledged—and, on top of that, what the burden of it was to mean, for Eliot himself, and more generally. The effort of the style is to hold together as one in wholeness through an apprehending consciousness that is also a moment of cultural *effort*, things that have been seen as separate. This, one might say, is what Eliot means, *really* means.

The forcefulness of Eliot's formulations has often been acknowledged, without, as far as I am aware, any attempt having been made to show what it is that makes the impression. The attempt has some bearing too, on what we mean when we say that Eliot's criticism is that of a poet: it at least deserves some of the attention we give to the poetry. The grammar is only superficially one of Johnsonian balance—since it never quite makes itself secure. It may *wish* to do so in its rhythms—but they only achieve a provisional security, with a suspended air, slightly prestidigitatory, in the clutter of phonemes (with the help of the alliterative touches) *sen, sen, time, tem, time, tem* . . . Only fancifulness would persist further than this: what can perhaps be said at last is that Eliot's grammar, here, is perfect for the expression of a certain tension, even strain. The two are one in a paradox of language: insecurity can be securely expressed—'while the music lasts'. For the sake, too, of the later argument one must stress the *active* nature of the achievement of these paragraphs (not, of course, of this one sentence alone) where elements are distinguished and defined, and then returned again to a position within a *sense* of the whole. The activity is an enactment, and it is parallel to what happens in some of the poetry; experience becomes thought, or, as D. W. Harding has said of the *Four Quartets*,[7] a 'concept is being created'—except, one would suggest, that what has been created has none of the finished-off, self-subsisting connotation of that word *concept*—a point that one would want to use to mark the difference between Eliot's critical notions and what has been made of them. Here we have a version of 'intellect at the tips of the senses'. Explication separates them.

It is a style that is both qualificatory and authoritative, and so quite unlike Johnson's. A truth is being worked out of sensation, and so the manner is not, it could not be, of the normal detached expository kind that can be written by the commentator without a personal stake in what he exposes. But we need not say at once that it is a *poet's* criticism only: a good deal of criticism written by men and women who are not 'poets', or are lesser poets, could be approached in the same way—that say of Blackmur, Burke,

Tate, Empson, or Leavis. It is the style of a critic to whom something means very much, personally—as ideas do also for some philosophers: Wittgenstein, Bradley, or Sartre.

Finally, this enactment is of what is being said: that the having of a full sense of the literary present and past is an *active* having; though Eliot's own phrase ('obtain by great labour') doesn't do justice to the free movement of his own prose at its best here and elsewhere. In these two paragraphs Eliot gets present and past into a proper relation, one that matches his own needs, with *his* needs, himself, in charge: *novelty* is better than repetition, the *new* work of art modifies 'the existing monuments', the 'supervention of novelty' alters, 'the whole existing order'. The weight is on the new life, and the present, although in the use of the word 'monument' one may feel the presence of an altar to the dead, a sense of fixity that can make the reader a little uneasy. In Eliot's essay 'there seems to be little feeling that a sense of tradition can be derived from the conditions of life round the poet . . . it is to be found in books.'[8]

Likewise, the use of *conform* in the second paragraph prefigures tendencies that do not really surface until the end of part I. Here the word conform does not quite fit with the rest of what is being said, and one can watch it being pushed, itself, into conformity with Eliot's own meaning. One may still wish for a different word, but then be glad that it was left. The imperfection is a key to what is going on, and induces a sympathy for the effort.

When we read the criticism of Johnson we experience an authority of another kind—the qualifications do not appear, in that way, in the surface of the prose. And that surface is most disinclined to crack in the way that Eliot's does, as we shall see. It is an authority that Eliot himself had mixed feelings about; something that might well be envied, but which it would be false to adopt in our times: 'a confidence so much stronger than any we can place in the style, or styles, of our own age that we can hardly see it as anything but a blemish upon his critical ability.'[9] It is something, however, that Eliot did on occasion adopt—a tone that critics have often properly objected to, one of his ventriloquisms. However, some critics, for example Chalker,[10] have used the word 'Johnsonian' to cover the general effects of the style of the critical essays. But to do this can only dull one's sense of the actual fluctions of tone, assimilating the best to the less good. To establish the difference between Eliot at his finest and Johnson, here is a well-enough known sentence of the latter's, from the opening of the 'Preface to Shakespeare'. It is of comparable length to the sentence from 'Tradition and the Individual Talent', and on a subject not so far from Eliot's own preoccupations:

> That praises are without reason lavished on the dead, and that the honours due only to excellence are paid to antiquity, is a complaint likely to be always continued by those, who, being able to add nothing to truth, hope for eminence from the heresies of paradox; or those, who being forced by disappointment upon consolatory expedients, are willing to hope from posterity what the present age refuses, and flatter themselves that the regard which is yet denied to envy, will be at last bestowed by time.[11]

This is something that Eliot's best reaches towards, but prevents itself from reaching—it would be a blemish if it were permitted. Eliot's sentence is cumulative and provisional; Johnson's, on the other hand, is substantive, and not only because of its more heavily nominal air. Counting the nouns will not tell us anything about that: it is, of course, the *kind* of nouns, the semantic weight they take from their age and the syntax with which they co-exist: it is all of a piece to the extent that one can say that the verbs in Johnson are drawn closer to the grammatical meaning of a noun: their aspect tends to the continuous, as in 'continued by those', 'willing to hope from', 'flatter themselves that'. Talking of past and future as he does ('antiquity and 'posterity' are established conceptions in a way that tradition is not) the verb frequently retreats from active to passive under their pressure. And at last, after the transition to the continuousness associated with hope, the passive returns—from the future (and the abstract)—upon the present. But the meaning of this passive is not one that you can find in grammar-books: it is particular to an age and a man. One might try and bridge the gap between criticism and linguistics by calling it the stoic-heroic passive, a near statis-tense, between past, present and future. It is something that Eliot, the apologist for Orthodoxy, is bound to have found enviable; his admiration perhaps reinforced by the sense of the need in Johnson which was met and fed by *his* time. It is where words like 'conform' and 'monument' point.

Eliot's present is not secure. He needs the past—Tradition and Orthodoxy—for support and confirmation in the face of the present, whereas Johnson confirms the past by the standards of his present. Both act out of the needs of the present; and though they may not be so dissimilar the relation of everything to everything else has shifted. Eliot's consciousness of change could not take this form:

> That praises are lavished on the dead
> > and
> that honours are paid to antiquity
> > > > is a complaint (etc.)
> by those who
> > being able to add nothing to truth
> > > hope for eminence from the heresies of paradox
> or those, who
> > being forced by disappointments (etc.)
> > > are willing to hope (etc.)
> > > and flatter themselves that
> > > > > the regard
> > > > > > which is yet denied to
> > > > > > envy
> > > > > > > will be at last bestowed by
> > > > > > > time.

The solid substance of parallels and the variation within them have their own keeping. Eliot's best is Eliot's, and Johnson's is Johnson's. It could not ever be true, as Professor Chalker says, that Eliot can sometimes 'pitch on exactly the same note'.[12] The passage he quotes comes from the essay on Seneca:

> An essential point to make about Seneca is the consistency of his writing, its maintenance on one level, below which he seldom falls and above which he seldom mounts ... Seneca is wholly himself; what he attempted he executed, he created his own genre.[13]

There are Johnsonian things there, but the opening is wholly of Eliot's own time; and the last comma is most un-Johnsonian (it might well have been thought 'ungrammatical' at the time), not really going with the weight of the preceding semi-colon. If, as Chalker says, the tone *was* 'immediately authoritative and magisterial' with 'a *gravitas* of syntax and phrasing', the more it was like Johnson the less it would be like Eliot's own voice in the paragraphs above, and the less it would convince.[14] To pitch on *exactly* the same note, in a different point in history, is to pitch on the wrong note if you have a different sort of voice. This does happen, and it is when Eliot is least himself, and allows another voice or voices to ventriloquize. On Thomas Hardy:

> He was indifferent even to the prescripts of good writing; he wrote sometimes overpoweringly well, but always very carelessly; at times his style touches sublimity without ever having passed through the stage of being good.[15]

It is not only Johnson who sounds there (though I don't wish to deny the quality of the remark). There is a fin-de-siècle wit about it, a touch of Oscar Wilde. The *individuality* of Eliot as we have discovered it, has begun to disappear. This, as we shall see, happens often enough to invite comment.

2

THE VOCABULARY OF EXTINCTION

However, to make anything like a thorough contrast of the best of Eliot with the best of Johnson is to draw out of one the recognition of the achievement of something distinctive and extremely fine. The failure in strength and solidity has its compensation in a heuristic seeking-for the lost authority. Something new is made—two of the best paragraphs of criticism in the twentieth century; the whole first part of the essay is a critical classic. There are many similar passages to honour in *The Sacred Wood* and the *Selected Essays*—and honouring them *includes* our perception of the difficulty of Eliot's historical position, for criticism and poetry, compared with that of the eighteenth century. It is just this perception that must affect the next comparison, of Eliot on Tradition with Eliot on Impersonality. Honest criticism of the latter must carry within it a sensitivity towards Eliot to the point where the necessity of saying just what the 'theory' of Impersonality means is properly balanced against the inevitable implication that must be made about the man who wrote it. That is how, at any rate, one would interpret the injunction about focussing on the poetry and not the poet. To see, too, that one cannot *help* making personal implications (criticism is never *so* pure), is to see that one is implicating oneself, and of the times in oneself. If they have changed since Eliot's time, they have not necessarily changed for the better, despite whatever advance there has been in English studies. One has a 'right to talk' only if that is recognized.

It is to complete his remarks on Tradition that Eliot feels he needs to add these paragraphs at the end of section I:

> What happens is a continual surrender of himself as he is at the moment to something which is more valuable. The progress of an artist is a continual self-sacrifice, a continual extinction of personality.
>
> There remains to define this process of depersonalization and its relation to the sense of tradition. It is in this depersonalization that art may be said to approach the condition of science. I therefore invite you to consider, as a suggestive analogy, the action which takes place when a bit of finely filiated platinum is introduced into a chamber containing oxygen and sulphur dioxide.

The next two paragraphs are the opening of section II, following directly on those above:

> Honest criticism and sensitive appreciation is directed not upon the poet but upon the poetry. If we attend to the confused cries of the newspaper critics and the susurrus of popular repetition that follows, we shall hear the names of poets in great numbers; if we seek not Blue-book knowledge but the enjoyment of poetry, and ask for a poem, we shall seldom find it. I have tried to point out the importance of the relation of the poem to other poems by other authors, and suggested the conception of poetry as a living whole of all the poetry that has ever been written. The other aspect of this Impersonal theory of poetry is the relation of the poem to its author. And I hinted, by an analogy, that the mind of the mature poet differs from that of

the immature one not precisely in any valuation of 'personality', not being necessarily more interesting, or having 'more to say', but rather by being a more finely perfected medium in which special, or very varied, feelings are at liberty to enter into new combinations.

The analogy was that of the catalyst. When the two gases previously mentioned are mixed in the presence of a filament of platinum, they form sulphurous acid. This combination takes place only if the platinum is present; nevertheless the newly formed acid contains no trace of platinum, and the platinum itself is apparently unaffected: has remained inert, neutral, and unchanged. The mind of the poet is the shred of platinum. It may partly or exclusively operate upon the experience of the man himself; but, the more perfect the artist, the more completely separate in him will be the man who suffers and the mind which creates; the more perfectly will the mind digest and transmute the passions which are its material.

The style, as well as the intent, of these paragraphs, when read and re-read, forces itself on one as something *quite different* from anything in part I. They show, I think, a deep incoherence that is not just a matter of a failure of 'argument'. As in a poem, the argument is not abstractable from the manner: *and yet* to say this entails the judgment that the incoherence, in style and argument, is all of a piece. The muddle is *organic* in the sense that it expresses a full but uncoordinated *need* of the personality—of Eliot's personality at this time—a need that cannot be consistently fulfilled. The intensity of the need is itself precisely a complement of the incoherence, and also of the deep, if obscurely moving, impression that this part of the essay makes upon the new reader—it is extremely hard to say *why*. Confusion contains intrinsic sets of double-binds:[16] the more you are in it, the more you want to get out of it; the more anxious you are to get out, the more anxiety assists confusion. It is something we have all experienced, in one way or another. This, I wish to argue, is at the root of the 'theory' of Impersonality—the apparatus of this part of the essay being an attempt to externalise. One can give some initial support to this somewhat contentious proposition by quoting Eliot himself on Baudelaire (it is characteristic of much of the most moving parts of his criticism that he transfers to others, or sees in others, reflections of his own preoccupations):

> the true claim of Baudelaire, as an artist, is not that he found a superficial form, but that he was searching for a form of life . . . he could, like anyone else, only work with the materials which were there . . . for such poets, one may expect often to get much help from reading their prose works, and notes and diaries; help in deciphering the discrepancies between head and heart, means and end, material and ideals.[17]

Likewise, Eliot could only work with the materials which were 'there'; in his perceptions of the needs of others is a near-clairvoyance into his own self: one might claim *this* as a perfectly proper impersonalisation.

It may be that the thought that there is an underlying sense amongst disorder is not common to literary criticism (being primarily interested in the justification of organic *wholes*); but it is to many varieties of psychological studies, and lies behind some of our commonest expressions—*I'm not my real self*, for example. Without the idea that *dis*order is an expression of the search for a lost order, a form of life, or a *wholeness* that might be found, such expressions could hardly justify themselves. However, psychology is not criticism, and the latter does not suffer from some of the disadvantages of the former:

> The most serious objection to the technical vocabulary used to describe psychiatric patients is that it consists of words which split man up verbally in a way which is analogous to the existential splits (in schizophrenic patients) we have described here. But we cannot give an adequate account of these unless we can begin from the concept of a unitary whole, and no such concept exists, nor can any such concept be expressed within the current language-system of psychiatry or psycho-analysis.[18]

Literary criticism has always had such a 'concept' of wholeness—and has not generally had to discover a scientific terminology for it. It has had more power perhaps for being understood without being expressed. We assume that the play, poem, novel is a whole if it is a success, that it will 'stand up to' analysis: we will not 'murder to dissect'. If a poem does not survive the attention of analysis it can be anything from somewhat wanting to being no poem at all. And criticism generally stops with the particular text —it does not cure anything except perhaps the corruption of literary taste; and it has defended this instinct against most psycho-analytic literary criticism which has dishonoured the traditional sense of wholeness in its demand for explanatory 'causes'. Criti-cism, where it is benevolent, wishes to honour the living whole that can even be made out of disordered life, or *a* disordered life. Perhaps, ideally, for criticism, people are like poems; as, for Milton, one should try to become 'the true poem'.

We may suspect a 'case' as a final cause of a literary failure; but the reasons *why* it is a failure are to be found within the text itself. The first and second kinds of explanation may indeed be con-nected, but we have no need to go beyond the latter. The in-coherence I wish to illustrate is first of all a literary variety, although it corresponds to both personal and cultural divisions, or splits; to deal with it as revealed in literature—though through a critical text usually only studied for its 'ideas'—is to deal, one hopes, with the tact of a proper respect for the other self: *manners*. So we can fulfil, but at the same time question, Eliot's require-ment for 'honest criticism and sensitive appreciation'.

The incoherence which is at the same time a searching for coherence is expressed in a number of ways within the essay—as disturbance may be expressed in eccentricities of behaviour. Content and expression are a whole, inseparable. But the original sin for criticism is that we must make some analytical separations in order to have anything to say: art is alone in trying to manifest truth in a single gesture. Here, 'Tradition and the Individual Talent' must be taken as expression and then as argument, and in that order so that the latter can be seen more clearly as part of the former: to abstract the theory and make sense of it, is to make something else of it.

A change occurs in the conduct of the essay at just about the point where Eliot himself divides it in order to discuss the idea of Impersonality directly, shifting the focus of the topic from the 'outer' concern (tradition) to the 'inner' one ('the process of depersonalization'). This change can be seen at once if we com-pare the opening three paragraphs of the extracts above with the

earlier confident manner, both qualificatory *and* authoritative.
They are peculiarly insecure.

A little of this impression can no doubt be accounted for in the
way that F. W. Bateson does, writing of the genesis of the essay
(which was published first in *The Egoist: An Individual Review*):[19]

> When the essay was reprinted in *The Sacred Wood* the text was
> left unchanged, the third sentence of the second part still begin-
> ning '*In the last article* I have tried to point out' (my italics). The
> words I have italicized were omitted in *Selected Essays* (1932),
> where one or two trivial verbal changes were also made, but
> the essay as we read it today remains otherwise exactly what
> the reader of the *Egoist* would have had in front of him in 1919.
> I stress the textual history of *Tradition and the Individual Talent*
> because it explains, if it does not excuse, the notorious episode
> of the finely filiated platinum.[20]

Bateson goes on to say that, searching for a catchy beginning and
end to the two main parts of the essay, Eliot, 'dipping desperately
into his memory' (Bateson doesn't say how he knows that Eliot
did that) bethought him of his 'stinks class' at school, and came
up with that 'episode'. This is interesting enough in a gossipy
kind of way, but what, actually does it 'explain'? It does not
explain *why* Eliot thought of a chemical analogy, and not some
other kind; nor does it explain why, having been used, the later
vocabulary of the essay remains in keeping with it, as we shall
see. It does not explain why, having done it, Eliot left it so long,
in reprinting after reprinting, of two different books: it is at least
a curious indifference from someone so fastidious: and that in
turn requires a *real* explanation. And it does not seem to occur to
Bateson himself, a steady defender of Eliot (as against Lawrence
and Leavis) and of the theory of Impersonality itself, that if this
part of the essay is so notorious then the actual importance of the
essay needs a very careful statement. The filiated platinum episode
is not, as a matter of fact, so easily detachable from the whole
second part of the essay: it cannot be 'explained' as a superficial
and somewhat inconsequent aberration. There is something a
good deal deeper here, which begins in the final paragraphs of
part I—and Eliot, having thought of his analogy, must have had

some time for second thoughts and modifications before the printing of the second part.

The awkwardness and repetitions are simply, one would have thought, too obvious for a writer of Eliot's standing to have left untouched; to have gone into the final form of a printed collection, if he had noticed or, if so, he had then cared. This begins with the introduction of the analogy upon which so much is to depend with the words 'I therefore invite you to consider'. We are left with the invitation, though, for a paragraph, which, however, couldn't be claimed to be a long time, if it contained more than a number of gestures towards being-just-about-to-begin, repetitions, rehearsals, glances towards tangential topics and so on—things that are or might be connected, but which the writing does not connect. 'And I hinted, by an analogy . . .' yes, but it was only a very short time ago, and Eliot speaks, or continues to speak, as if it was last week: the lecturer is preparing his class for today's instalment. It has very much the air of being stuck on. Moreover, he has already given us a considerable amount of the analogy, and he gives it to us again later. This may seem to be the mere correcting of superficialities, except that the change of tone consists with other matters, a deeper insecurity. Furthermore, it is not that there is a single change of tone: there are fluctuations through several.

These start with the apparently confident assertion of concentrated principle in the first sentence. But then the second shifts, not to an expansion of the principle (perhaps in answer to the question *Why?*), but to a parallel matter: what things are like nowadays. Eliot points away to something else, and rather too suddenly. In so far as an argument is being followed here (it is in fact rather more like another analogy) it only amounts to saying that we ought to be able to see that A is true because newspaper criticism is the reverse. It is, in short, a sub-class of question-begging. On top of that, it goes with a tone that is defensive-aggressive. It is that underlying motive that the pomposity serves. This is not the authoritative Eliot, nor even the Johnson-imitative, but the sermonical-superior.

'*If we attend to*'—well, of course, you and I wouldn't usually, but if we *can* bring ourselves down from our superior position; '*the susurrus of popular repetition*'—the long word, as so often with

Eliot ('obnubilation' is another case) indicates a reflex of defensive hauteur; *we shall hear . . . in great numbers*—here the tone veers towards the sermon, then, with *if we seek not . . . and ask for . . . we shall seldom find it'*, it begins to encompass the Biblical. Somewhere, there is a recollection of bread and stones.

This is quite out of keeping with the assertion of principle, and with the offer to define scientifically—with the surrounding intentions and vocabulary. The tone could only be acceptable if it were deliberately comic or consistently parodistic. But the context won't permit it and consequently it can't be anything settled. And the reader's feeling that Eliot has not got hold of what it is that he wants to say is confirmed by Eliot himself, here and later, with his 'I have tried to point out', 'I have hinted . . .', 'the point of view I am struggling to attack . . .', 'in the light—or darkness—of these observations'. He is struggling, and at length the reader who has not allowed himself to be frightened into aquiescence will sooner or later ask himself: What is all this *for*?

Repetitions and instability of tone are joined in this part of the essay by an inclination to advance the argument by a method of appositional shifts—another variety of question-begging.[21] Things are brought together, but not properly *connected*; and this is the case whether what is brought in is lengthy (as in the example of the catalyst) or brief. Consider the second sentence of the examples on page 42, where the shift is entirely characteristic but expresses a hidden intention rather more openly than some:

> The progress of an artist is a continual self-sacrifice, a continual extinction of personality.

The ideas of *sacrifice* and *extinction* are brought together as if they were interchangeable synonyms. *But they aren't.* To sacrifice the self you have to have one to sacrifice, and for the sacrifice to continue the self must persist—it is after all a normal assumption of normal human beings that (somehow or other) they are as it were continuous with themselves: the child is father of the man. But extinction is not, for all that, *continual*, an idea that readily dissociates from finality. One can sacrifice oneself without extinction: what, it might be asked, would be the value to God of extinction? It is something that Christianity has always enjoined against. And the phrase cannot be defended on the ground that here Eliot is using the word 'personality' in his special way; for if *sacrifice* and *extinction* are synonyms, so, obviously, are *personality* and *self*, here. And finally, the whole idea is an implicit contradiction of the remark earlier in part I, that novelty is better than repetition. Extinction could hardly lead to anything more than the perpetuation of those monuments—in a kind of literary cemetery. If the personality was actually extinguished in the moment of poetic creation, what would one be bringing to the past?

The main part of the explanation of this apposition is that the two terms come from different vocabularies, one of them specialized, the other one not. The exchange of these two terms, the false synonym, must be the nub of my criticism of the essay, concentrating for us as they do so much that follows, not merely illustrating the way in which Eliot can manipulate an elision between things that don't fit. The first vocabulary is essentially religious-metaphysical: 'surrender', 'ideal order', 'temporal', 'timeless', and so on. The second vocabulary is scientific.[22] This latter is almost absent from part I. In the second part we change, as it were, from divergence to convergence, as Eliot turns inwards to the psychological aspect of tradition which is Impersonality. Extinction goes with 'depersonalization', 'process', 'define', 'medium', 'digest', 'material', 'elements', 'added to', 'use', 'obtained by', 'suspension', 'receptacle', 'unite', 'compound', 'pressure', 'particles', 'employs', and of course (the germ of it all) 'catalyst', and so on. In such a context words which come from, or can be easily used in other contexts take on a tinge from the whole—even 'use' becomes scientific *use*. Moreover, these terms go with the scientific lecturer's tone of voice, which sorts so strangely with the cleric's[23] 'I invite you to consider', 'the action which takes place', 'I hinted', 'you will notice' (in our detached way), 'if you compare'. The tone is of course very much continuous with the catalyst analogy which is used as the basis of the subsequent 'theory' (the word is inevitably elevated from more general to more particular meaning) of poetic creativity.

This change has of course been commented on, but not in a way, I think, which takes in its significance properly. F. W. Bateson's use of the word 'notorious' is a recognition of some of that comment and yet, characteristically (and not just of Bateson), what he is referring to is just the catalyst 'episode' as if that could be isolated from the rest of this part of the essay. Take too, *this* interesting quotation from an early review of Eliot's prose which starts by praising Eliot for his genuine disinterestedness. But what kind of disinterestedness is it?:

> of science, as opposed to the pseudo-science of the literary-criticism-brand-of-psychology-type . . . The sense in reading that every word in every sentence is significant . . . derives from Mr. Eliot's desire to circumscribe exactly the situation he is dealing with . . . The central ideas, of 'Impersonality' and of 'the historical sense', are of the same kind as scientific hypotheses; . . . principles of investigation . . . the author of *Tradition and the Individual Talent* was an empiricist. The apparent large-scale logical cohesion of the essay dissolves away on close inspection. Although the argument has the appearance of being the work of a distinguished theoretician examining the specific case, it turns out to be the great experimentalist turning over his results to the student.[24]

Science is the measure, and there is little doubt that it is a useful measure of a certain kind of scrupulousness and disinterestedness. As a part of cultural history it has had to be reckoned with, and the effect has shown in criticism—particularly in I. A. Richards' work. But we might at least suggest to ourselves that, as with so many cultural influences, we have come to give it an almost unconscious assent, as if we thought that, 'objectivity' belonging to it, we surrendered all other measure to it.[25] Winkler praises—and blames—according to the measure, and only according to it. He looks in the one direction, and is unaware of others. Just as Eliot hands himself over to scientific vocabulary, Winkler attaches himself to the scientific view of things. And because they are both within the same enclosure of assumptions Winkler cannot see certain things: his field of vision is restricted, as is that of exegetical-theoretical criticism. He can't see the difference between the two parts of the essay, as we have already noted them. How is it that Eliot's 'desire' for exactness 'dissolves away' like that? To ask that question—Winkler doesn't—would mean expelling oneself from one's own assumptions. In order to stay within them, and explain his feeling of general dissatisfaction with Eliot's essay, Winkler has to find a distinction between theory and experiment which is simply nonsense. For (a) Science does *not* value theory above experiment, and (b) there is no reason to make a connection, implied here, between a lack of logical cohesion and the doing of experiments—if anything, the reverse. And what experiment could Eliot carry out—is Winkler taking Eliot's tone ('I invite you to consider . . .') seriously? The answer must be on the whole, yes; for his essay is really of a piece with Eliot's own: a matter of analogies and metaphor, but without the substance that can only be given *by doing science*.

Eliot's employment of his own 'analogy' is similar in its underlying intention and effect to the other previously noticed 'shifts' in tone, and between terms. An analogy *is* a variety of apposition, a form of metaphorical synonym. This (placed here) is like, or the same as, that (placed there). Things are put or said side-by-side—and there are good ways of doing this—or you can cheat, or mislead yourself if you don't suspend belief *in* the analogy. For example, atoms can be thought to be like billiard balls, usefully, only if we know at the same time that they are not. In scientific popularization, of course, the movement is away from the un-visualizable abstract towards common experience. Eliot's is from the obscure but immediate experience (which no one has 'explained') towards the securities of scientific language and description. A scientific analogy is a reference to a special variety of the impersonal, one sanctioned by the common experience of *experiments*. And so the description (Eliot very significantly uses the word 'define'—but he doesn't 'define') cannot help but give an extremely strong impression of certitude. And this certitude transfers itself easily—more than that, it is precisely continuous *with*—the assertions, just as he previously shifted from assertion to appeal at the beginning of section II, and from sacrifice to extinction before that. The appositions, one might say are 'like' equations. The tactic is consistent in this part of 'Tradition and the Individual Talent'; the argument is not *really* scientific and, not being what it seems to be, it still cannot be another kind of argument. (A fruitful comparison here, if we need to look farther than the essay itself, would be Coleridge's 'definition' of Imagination in *Biographia Literaria*.) Analogy and assertion combine in the phrase 'The mind of the poet is the shred of platinum': the words 'inert, neutral, and unchanged' transfer themselves from one side of Eliot's equation to the other. The mind of the poet *is* what it is said to be by virtue of the honorific connotations of the language of science. There is nothing heuristic about this, nor anything biographically 'open'.[26] This way of talking, too, goes with (or should go with) experiments that have been done. Eliot is talking about something, the mind of the poet, on which no experiments have been done, or could be—no poet in his right 'mind' would let you.

None of this should be taken to suggest, of course, that Eliot has no warrant for writing about this subject at all. He has had the experience of writing poems, and can tell us some of the things that happen. The style of the first part of the essay is the expression of one way of reflecting upon that experience, and that style, as we have seen, is entire, characteristic, individual, that of a particular man. The manner of part II, however, is none of those things; and where it has a consistency it is that of no man, but a method. In the first part Eliot writes as a matter of conviction and belief, and our confidence, our belief, is established and sustained by the expression. When he talks about Impersonality, he tries to extinguish himself in an impersonal vocabulary—with the result that he achieves only fragmentary ventriloquisms (is it not odd that Eliot should discuss the creation of wholes (poems) in such a manner?) or a language in actual contradiction with the subject. For if poetic making, as Eliot frequently claims, is largely sub-conscious:

> I don't believe that the relation of a poem to its origins is capable of being very clearly traced ... if, either on the basis of what poets try to tell you, or by biographical research, with or without the tools of the psychologist, you attempt to explain a poem, you will probably be getting further and further away from the poem without arriving at any other destination.[27]

and if it needs to stay so, then it can't be known. But the language that owes its existence to the doing that is science is there to express the known. Science only in certain circumstances needs to 'use similitudes'[28] for the obscure or the unknown; it is too easy to tempt ourselves into believing that we know things that we don't. Eliot has a natural warrant for talking about these matters, which is the same as that of a priest to talk about ghostly matters; but he has no warrant for talking in this way. And if *he* has not, nor has any one of us.

The main index of this curious dissociation of language with subject occurring in this section of 'Tradition and the Individual Talent' is the scientific terminology:[29] Eliot, writing about something that *must* be personal turns to an impersonality to express it, as if to bear out the word extinction, as against sacrifice. But the language of science is a specialized one, in so far as it is valid only when it is attached to experiment or data done or collected, from which we can continue other attempts at verification and falsification. But if a poem cannot be repeated, if every creative act is different, then the method of repetition ('what only a genius could do yesterday, any fool can do today') cannot be applied, and the language is inappropriate in itself as well as being discontinuous with the different 'register' of part I. Eliot does talk about the poet (his language makes him) *as if* he had done an experiment, *as if* experience was experiment, and *as if* this was generalizable. He has only a metaphor—which becomes an assumption, the assumption is expressed as assertion. Language becomes a mask.

The last word has to lead us to propose a connection with the other 'languages' or momentary tones that flicker within Eliot's critical style (the one consistency is the inconsistency, *throughout his career*): the Johnsonian-authoritative, the sermonising, the scientific lecturer's, the academician's, the class-snobbish:

> . . . the possessors of the inner voice ride ten in a compartment to a football match at Swansea, listening to the inner voice, which breathes the eternal message of vanity, fear, and lust.[30]

('Why Swansea?' as a student of my own, from Swansea, once innocently asked.) These are not Eliot's own voice—we have seen what that sounds like—they are ventriloquisms, where the relation to the speaker is ambiguous (and has its own curiosity and fascination, therefore)—something is sitting on his knee. Who is *really* talking—can this *really* be taken as truth? The paradox that is embedded, in the ambiguity, of course, is that one reveals (one's own fears, as above) as one masks. In poetry the persona—in Tennyson, Browning, Pound and Eliot—*can* work well in this

5

way where it is consistently sustained throughout a particular piece. (The modern need for *persona* seems to be something quite distinctive.)[31] But this is not consistent, nor is it poetry. We are bound to ask ourselves—when a man is talking in this way, to what extent can we take it as *him* speaking; to what extent did he 'believe in' this theory; what status can such a theory have; what sense should be made of it? Certainly, the 'abstractable ideas' have to be connected back to the need—and to say that is to insist on a wholeness of declaration which the necessary 'de-personalization' of science and its language can't be accommodated to. To achieve a wholeness you have to understand the need itself, fully: how it has arisen in you and in your times. Eliot's finest perceptions are provisional—it is one of the things that gives them their peculiar intensity.

In short, we can know as much now from Eliot's own career in poetry and criticism as from the metaphysical poets or from cultural history, what 'dissociation of sensibility' can mean. It may, therefore, strike us as odd enough to require an explanation (if we think that the new philosophy which put all in doubt had something to do with that dissociation) that Eliot can so easily turn to this language, or so easily and unconvincingly turn a *bon-mot* from Pater: 'It is in this depersonalization that art may be said to approach the condition of science'. But the essay on the metaphysical poets was to come two years later: at this stage we can merely mark what happens in the earlier essay as an unconsciousness; and it may well be that a fuller consciousness—the 'theory' of the dissociation of sensibility is hardly more than an uncompleted gesture—was impossible at the time.

3

THE LOGIC OF DIVISION

But if the second part of 'Tradition and the Individual Talent' is not stylistically coherent, could it be, nevertheless, coherent as argument? Does one incoherence entail another, or can we assume that the levels of discourse can be separated, and the 'content' taken out? There are a number of difficulties in trying to do the latter.

The first of these might be called *epistemological*. The logical problem here is directly connected with the choice of style, as the style implies a mode of knowing. An analogy is one thing; but to go on talking *from within it* is another. Phrases like 'it may exclusively operate upon' (the experience of the man himself), 'digest and transmute material' carry the connotations of an external and objective knowledge into an area where, as we have seen, it is difficult for them to apply. How does Eliot know that this is the way that the 'mind of the poet' works? To convince he would have to tell us things that he doesn't; three kinds of things—what others have said, observations of himself, or critical analysis of passages. But there is none of this: Eliot proposes to give a 'definition' without having given any kind of *description*. The nearest he comes to it is in his pointing to examples, where it is said that they show certain things, without their being presented for us, so that Eliot's statements that this *was* so, that such and such 'came', that this did that, but not this, recoil upon a probably ('was probably in suspension') which still can raise itself up to a 'fact' ('the poet's mind is in fact a receptacle for seizing').[32] These facts are metaphors, supposition and assertion disguised in an objective style.

This difficulty, having to do with a kind of knowledge, is very closely connected to the second—a peculiar variety of *intentionalism*. Eliot continues to talk—about Homer, Dante and Shakespeare —as if they all 'worked' in the same way, the neutral and combining way which, one supposes, is derived from his own experience. But how does he know? Eliot clearly has a warrant, as a *matter of belief* for saying that this is so for him; but without the kind of support mentioned before—a scientist would say—the warrant is only good for explorations of himself—and those require a different language. He has no access to others' experience. It may be a consciousness of this that draws him into his inverted intentionalism:

> The episode of Paolo and Francesca employs a definite emotion, but the intensity of the poetry is something quite different from whatever intensity in the supposed experience it may give the impression of.

and

> ... the murder of Agamemnon, or the agony of Othello, give an artistic effect apparently closer to a possible original than the scenes from Dante.[33]

Beside the superficial tentativeness of 'possibly', 'supposed' and 'apparently' stands the certitude of 'something *quite* different' and '*definite* emotion'. By them we are forced to ask the question—how can he possibly know that the intensity of the emotion is different, if he does not know (he virtually says that he does not) what that experience is? Eliot's *anti*-personal theory expresses itself here quite differently from that of Wimsatt and Beardsley's famous essay 'The Intentionalist Fallacy', to which the mind automatically turns: 'we ought to impute the thoughts and attitudes of the poem immediately to the dramatic speaker, and if to the author at all, only by a biographical act of inference.'[34] Eliot does not give us that—nor would a biographical act of inference necessarily help, here—for he is not talking about a *process* that has become conscious, and might be expressed, but one which is unconscious, intervening between two quite different things, an emotion and a poem. We neither know the process that changed the original emotion, nor that emotion itself. Yet Eliot can say that things are quite different. Secondly, Wimsatt and Beardsley's rigour cuts the poem right off from the creator: their 'science of objective evaluation' is separate from 'the psychology of composition'. For aesthetic reasons they wish to stop criticism having it both ways and focus on the verbal object or 'icon'—to stop a confusion once and for all. And one feels that their severity is sometimes such as to prevent us from projecting even reasonable positive possibilities from the poem outwards, to connect with a biography we can't help knowing. Eliot on the other hand projects negative deductions: nothing that is in the poem, *because* it is different, can tell him what the difference is. To know that A is different from B, you have to know both A and B. And he doesn't know what Dante's and Shakespeare's emotion was, here—he gets away with saying so by his 'supposed' and his 'possible'. This is tautology and solipsism at once. Eliot cannot show that experience and creation are separate, and consequently has *no non-analogical foundation* for the famous dictum that, 'the more perfect the artist, the more completely separate in him will be the man who suffers and the mind which creates'.

Nor, it should be emphasized, has he any personal foundation by which he might convince us, since he has adopted the language of an objective impersonality. To be able to say that these things are different, you would have to assume just the reverse of what he says—that the two things are connected in him, that he knows both, knows them to be connected, but not the same. Eliot, as a consequence of his general position, has to maintain a false appearance of knowing,[35] dependent on his authority as a poet— a kind of biographical authority of position (always insecure) and not of person, without any biographical revelation or any of the particular strength that comes from the personal.

A third, also connected (but minor) difficulty is that we are offered explanations which have the appearance of being conclusive (it is another effect of the adopted terminology), and yet Eliot consistently refers to the unknown, an unknown which it is another tendency of his argument to want to retain. Stead in *The New Poetic* remarks that the essay 'consistently opposes' two sets of terms of which one refers, roughly, to rational actions of the mind, the other to the more irrational, the conscious to the unconscious, personality to (one meaning of) impersonality. And Stead remarks rightly that 'the escape from personality which Eliot describes in this essay is not an escape from self, but an escape *further into the* self. The concern of the essay is, in fact, a desire to release the poet from his own rational will.'[36] It goes with this desire of course that Eliot constantly speaks of the poet's mind as being a medium, a receptacle for things that 'come' and 'enter into combinations'.

There must therefore be an essential contradiction between apparent purpose and underlying motive in this. It is not that the unconscious *can't* be talked about rationally, even 'scientifically': it can, well, or badly, though more easily by someone other than oneself, from the 'outside' rather than 'inside'. Things can be brought up to the surface and explanations given if one has a strong enough will to self-exposure. But this can only be done where the intention is to do so, to release unconscious motive to rational scrutiny. Eliot, as a critic, must speak rationally (and on this subject that would entail exposure) and try to explain relations. But Eliot the poet-in-the-critic (but why should we not say Eliot the man in the face of this co-presence?) wants to retain his avenue of escape deep into the self. So connections must be severed: you can't tell people where you have gone and go and hide there. Eliot offers to explain what he does not *want* to explain;[37] logic, reason, become apparent or occasional, dualisms develop, splits are maintained by style, one thing will not go with another.

Eliot's *dualisms*[38] do not arise primarily from a conscious resolve to explain a problem of knowing: they arise from this split of motive. The most famous division of the personality into parts separates the man who suffers from the mind which creates. So says the critic, who is presumably the man, and not the poet. But if the man includes the critic, the critic knows, or claims to know, about the poet. He might be felt to be intermediate—one might see the words as indicating connections, activities of the man rather than essences within him: 'the poet' generalizes, abstracts (in the two senses of the word) and assimilates. One can read what Eliot says, in one way, as indicating a sense that it is a matter of degree ('more completely separate') and then go on and say, as Marx did, that sufficient difference in degree makes difference in kind; but that is a separate argument, and it is not there. But as we have seen, Eliot's motive is towards separation, which his vocabulary constantly reflects.

Having expressed separation rather than connection, some curious things happen. The analogy of the catalyst suggests that *one* thing (sulphurous acid) is formed from *two* things (gases). This is transferred to the creation of *one* thing (poem) from *one* thing (experience). One is about to murmur about the scientific impossibility of that when Eliot divides experience into elements of his own, 'emotions' and 'feelings' (and his 'you will notice' is a way of stilling the question 'What's the difference?'—we should *know*, even though it is the first time it has been mentioned). But,[39] he goes on to say, at the same time, poetry 'may be formed out of one emotion, or may be a combination of several', or it may be formed 'without any emotion whatsoever: composed out of feelings solely'. The catalyst can make something out of one thing, or out of things that are the same kind of thing, not different, as with the gases, or with the presumed difference between feeling and emotion. The scientific precision of the analogy proves to have a very loose connection with the subsequent description.

This again can only be explained as the reflection of the double motives—to explain, and not to—which the scientific method of analysis by the persistent automatic division of wholes into parts ideally satisfies. But ironically, it is the physicist who has the conception of the *whole*—the atom, or the electron, or the particle even—which Eliot, with all his moving anxiety through poetry and criticism to 'bring into balance the two halves of the divided sensibility' (Stead) has not. He *starts* from a division: the physicist starts from the whole.

This becomes clearer through Stead's useful, *very* useful, listing of the key words in the three essays in 'Tradition' (1919) and 'Hamlet' (1919), and 'Ben Jonson' (1919). These words, Stead says, 'may be arranged in this way':[40]

'impersonal'	'personal'
'unconscious'	(conscious) 'mind'
'feelings'	'emotions'
'images, phrases'	'structure'
'detail'	'design'

they are 'set consistently in opposition to one another'; and they express the possibility of a dualism in almost every aspect of temperament. (Just to be able to arrange things in such a way is also an expression of the assumption.)[41] Distinction upon distinction is made—some requiring 'definition'—between elements—sensation, feeling, emotion. Vincent Buckley has made a detailed listing of some of the baffling questions that Eliot's use of 'feeling' and 'emotion' can produce in the close reader of Eliot's text, and concludes: 'From first to last, he distinctly separates feeling and emotion but he never clearly distinguishes their natures.'[42] And for all that things are 'clear' to F. W. Bateson:

> . . . it has often been assumed that by feeling Eliot meant emotion . . . [but] it is clear that *here* [Bateson quotes 'the elements which enter the presence of the transforming catalyst are of two kinds: emotions and feelings'] as elsewhere in Eliot's early critical writings, *feeling* means sensation. And the sensibility is the faculty . . . ' (etc.)[43]

for all that, one has only to ask oneself whether one is actually clearer oneself, to put it all back into a muddle. Would any number of new words such as he proposes make it all easier—for all of which we could ask for definitions? What sort of sensations might they be? The only distinctions we make between these words are those we can detect in ordinary use, and *those* are not consistent. In all of this there are *dictionary* definitions, but no final scientific ones (if even they are quite final) of the kind that we have for *ohm* or *catalyst*. And suppose one should pick up the usage of Yeats, in a letter to Olivia Shakespeare, describing a sequence of poems he was writing as 'all emotion, and impersonal'. It might well send one back to the beginning again, or tempt one to give up altogether.

But it is not just the great difficulty of trying to express the differences between the significance of words like these (how do we know that one is one and not the other, when we have one of them—was that a feeling, or an emotion, or a sensation, or a — ?) that makes us uneasy, as if we were splitting and naming internal atoms; it is also that, if we are to take them seriously, how do we explain their acting *together*? Analysis, dualism, classification can revenge themselves, if they cannot help us to explain the wholeness of the result: the piece of work that is a man, or a poem.

It is normal in ordinary language to use the words person, personality, personal (excluding those uses which indicate 'false' or 'acting' or 'role'—selves, as in 'TV personality') to express our sense of unique wholeness of character. Anything we see as 'impersonality' we see as an aspect of the larger conception, existing by virtue of, and within, a particular individuality. Eliot's use of the word-pair alters the ordinary relation of the terms from one of primary and subordinate terms, to one of equivalence; and we must feel that this is connected with the impulse towards extinction and de-personalisation (there is something distasteful in the use) along with the inclination, even in part I, to conformity.

4

The general need for a serious interest in artistic—and moral—detachment, submission, selflessness, disinterestedness, *imper-*

sonality, is as clear, or even clearer, today as it was in Eliot's own time of writing. The self-expression that is simply self-indulgence or self-deception in any aspect of life is the persisting artistic sin. And in part I of his essay Eliot states the conditions for a correction as well as they have ever been stated. There, the style is consistent and individual, and goes with the burden of the argument that the impersonality is the result of a continuous *active* exchange[44] between poet-present and the past of the tradition. Novelty stands against conformity, submission against assertion. The second section is radically at odds with this, except that its contrasting *passivity* (expressed in part by the acceptance of styles not his own) connects with the air of effort, of weariness, of part I. In the one case the poet, like anyone else, is shaped through the perpetual collision of self with what is not the self in a persistent assertion and submission—it is no wonder that in Eliot's times, as in our own, this might seem a matter involving labour, struggle, 'sweating', difficulty and responsibility, an unhappy condition of the double-edged privilege of being a poet.[45] It is enough to make one sympathetic to what happens in section II—for where else *can* one place one's explanation for it but within the personality of Eliot himself? He *hopes* that through passivity, neutrality, inertness, those permanent moments of impersonality might be achieved that we call poems. There seems to be no external reason, nor reason in argument, why this latter should not have been the meaning given to the word impersonality; and so where else can one look for an explanation of what does happen to the essay, but inward, to Eliot's own needs—an impulse to escape from 'the intolerable wrestle with words and meanings'. The word 'escape' (used also in a peculiarly neutral way by Stead) occurs in contexts, the effect of which is to produce in the reader that peculiar contradictory tug between sympathy and rejection, corresponding to the powerful undertow of emotion disguising itself under a surface-style of confident assertion (it is one of the things which bring about the peculiar fascination of the essay):

> Poetry is not a turning loose of emotion, but an escape from emotion; it is not the expression of personality, but an escape from personality. But, of course, only those who have

personality and emotions know what it means to want to escape from those things.[46]

The words 'personality' and 'emotion' here are used in two ways —but the shift is not very obvious. In the first sentence the semantic connection is still with 'the surface mind' (Stead), something insufficient in itself, to be repudiated—though it may help to provide design or structure in poem or play. The second use shifts it away towards life. And the tone of that sentence is ambiguous—'it is only people like me, who have (strong) emotions, a (strong) personality, who are really in a position to tell the rest of you, who don't have these things' (can he really mean that?—but what else?) 'what it means'. It is hard not to read this as a boast—our whole 'common language judgement'[47] is on the side of that. Except, one might say, that at the bottom of the preceding page Eliot has remarked that 'It is not in his personal emotions . . . that the poet is in any way remarkable or interesting'. That might neutralize the boast, but at the same time it must presumably make the poet like anyone else, in which case the class of those who knows what it means to escape from these things is very much enlarged from the group which is apparently privileged to possess something they would in any case want to *escape* from. No *sense* can be made of this at all; it can only be *explained*, by saying that something in Eliot prevents him from being consistent according-ing to the impersonal standards of reason and argument. A buried and disordering emotion that he can't escape from breaks the surface in the accents of self-pity.

It has to be said that part II of 'Tradition and the Individual Talent' is itself an escape, from the implications of part I; and that in so far as it is an escape, it is sentimental. To resist the unbridled effusions of the surface personality, you don't need to escape— you only need to bridle yourself.[48] And one cannot help connect-ing the sentimentality with the inclination to speak too easily of 'aesthetic' as opposed to 'historical' criticism (p. 15) and of 'purely literary values, the appreciation of good writing for its own sake'.[49] These things too can be escapes, sentimentalities. And when one has seen that, it is hard to resist the contrast with the earlier remark that the poet who is aware of the relation of the past and the pre-sent 'will be aware of great difficulties and responsibilities'.

The word 'impersonality' in 'Tradition and the Individual Talent' points in opposing ways, just as the two halves of the essay do not go together: the religious connotations—*active*—are at odds with the feat of pseudo-scientific legerdemain—*passive*. But a further meaning is part of the active side of the essay, a meaning that is of the style in its achievement of a vital accommodation between the individual and the Johnsonian. It is a meaning that, too, is of the best poems: a new whole, or wholeness has been made, distinctive and apart-from the maker, impersonal in that sense. It is precisely by such a struggle of *relation* that the very thing Eliot was looking for is created. It cannot be avoided; Eliot said it couldn't be avoided—and then he went on to try to avoid it. He has to be judged by his own standards, which he cannot escape. To try to escape from them was to slip towards the conventionality of orthodoxy as expressed, for example, in *After Strange Gods*. For although 'experiences which seem to go unusually deep often have the temporary effect on the individual of an emptying out of all personality'[50] the effect *is* only temporary, and the living struggle resumes. The alternatives are extinction, or dogmatism: but they could be the same thing.

CHAPTER III

Personality and the Proper Relation

Since 'Tradition and the Individual Talent' appeared, a great deal of critical attention has been focussed on the significance; the extensions, personal, cultural and philosophical of 'impersonality': what the word might mean, and why such a theory was necessary at all. But there is comparatively little to be found, on the other hand, about Eliot's use of the companion-word, 'the necessary opposite'. In Mildred Martin's bibliography,[1] for example, there are a number of references to *impersonality*, but none to *personality*. A significant absence. And it would, I think, be difficult to discover an individual critical enquiry[2] into Eliot's use *of* the term, though there are many about his attitude *towards* it, derived from the particular and peculiar sense given to it in 'Tradition'. But the word is scattered so freely throughout his whole critical output, and in such a variety of contexts (it occurs far more frequently than *impersonality*), that it deserves similar attention on its own account.

Perhaps one reason for this absence may be that the word is simply assumed as the ground against which a new and curious use, stands out; and which as a consequence we find it difficult to look at at all. When we read, something may happen to us similar to, but not *the same* as, what Owen Barfield has suggested we can see in medieval literature, philosophy and art: we too obey assumptions so fundamental that they are culturally unconscious. Indeed, without some such unconsciousness we might find it hard to get along:

In the work of Thomas Aquinas, in particular, the word *participate* or *participation* occurs almost on every page, and a whole book could be written—indeed one has been written— on the uses he makes of it. It is not a technical term of philosophy

and he is no more concerned to define it than a modern philosopher would be to define some such common tool of his thought
as, say, the word *compare*.[3]

Our own world, likewise, takes things for granted; and so, likewise again, does critical theory: thoughtless habits of thought.
But a figure does not exist without the ground; and therefore we
might ask what it is that the theory of Impersonality stands out
against: what common attitudes might make it appear eccentric?
The appearance of the conception, at this time, in these places (in
France and England: in Hulme, Pound, Yeats and Joyce; modified
into doctrines of *persona* and *mask*)[4] and then the subsequent
fading-away of a primary interest in it may in the longer run
come to appear as a momentary inversion of more normal
assumptions about personality. At that moment Lawrence was
saying that 'the time to be impersonal has gone. We start from
the joy we have in being ourselves . . .'[5]
    What happens to Eliot's uses of *personality* under the influence
of *impersonality*? The two terms go together, after all: there is no
conception of the one without the other. We would therefore
expect that the characteristics of the theory of Impersonality
would reflect on *personality*. If one word means something special,
then so will the other: it is unavoidable within the universe of
relations that makes up language at any one moment. Neither
personality nor *impersonality* is the fundamental conception: *that* is
impersonality-personality, something lying beyond each individual word to which they point, together. The relation is like that
of a function in mathematics, but more complex—a change in the
one implies a change in the other, as consumption of fuel varies
with speed. However, the matter is *far* more complex, since each
variable here contains an undefined chain of others. The question
therefore becomes one of consistency: Is Eliot's alteration of
ordinary usage consistent? Does it maintain itself? If one or the
other of the terms between the play of which Eliot's purpose is
sustained is unstable, then the whole will become unstable. And
there can be no doubt that Eliot's limitation on our ordinary uses
of the word '*personality*' so that he could bring it into something
like an antithetical relation to *impersonality* (as a presumed virtue)
does do violence to the natural scope of the term. It is not unfair,

even at this early point in the argument, to quote Hulme: 'the fundamental error is that of placing perfection in humanity, thus giving rise to that bastard thing Personality, and the bunkum that follows from it.'[6]

To do what Eliot tries to do means that the two terms must be regarded as of equal weight—personality: impersonality. And one can see this happening in some parts of the criticism. *Personality* means only false self-expression, critically unchecked, sentimental. This deliberate limitation is enforced and then held in place by the motive to exalt the opposite term (which in turn, as we have seen, is reduced to a special *sense*). Eliot's primary interest is in the secondary term (*impersonality*)—an interest largely, but by no means wholly, entailed by the poetic circumstances of his own time. It might be said, one supposes, that if this special use was firmly held in its antithetical relation, the reader would not feel uneasy with it; there would not be too much sense of dislocation. We would have something like the deliberate limitation of scientific terms; a reductive, but precise, meaning within the context. But how long could one maintain that against an ordinary-language use? Is the context specialised enough? Moreover—does Eliot do it? Our ordinary use embodies a common-language judgment—and this is not a poem, where meanings may be differently '*eingeschachtelt*'. If Eliot's own range of uses should prove not to be consistent, what might this tell us about the endeavour? Is it necessary for Eliot to go against the common use?

In our common-language judgment, *impersonality* is the secondary form—one of those unconscious assumptions that conscious sense enforces. The negative cannot exist without the positive. The idea of personality is semantically precedent even if, admittedly, the case is not quite the same as for *good* and *bad*, where the words, the 'concepts', are entirely dependent, and therefore of equal weight (except insofar as good is valued more highly). You cannot have too much good, or too little bad. But we *do* say that someone has too much personality (as also cleverness) or is too impersonal: both conceptions contain the possibility of a negative, whereas *good* and *bad* don't. But still, while the nature of his terms gives Eliot *some* warrant for his dislocation of common use, the relation between them is ineluctable: this particular assumption is more than (in Barfield's terms) cultural. There are grounds for using that much-abused word *existential*:

> In the scheme of the personal ... a positive contains and is constituted by its own negative ... The impersonal attitude in a personal relation is the negative which is necessarily included in the positive personal attitude, and without which it could not exist ... in a personal relation between persons an impersonal relation is necessarily included and subordinated. The negative is for the sake of the positive. Or ... we may say that the relation is intentionally personal, and includes the impersonal as a matter of fact.[7]

This idea of personality, from which impersonality is abstracted, is, or rather, *has* to be, 'a principle of unity and a principle of continuity'[8] however impossible it may be to express that principle.

Is there then, perhaps, an instability in Eliot's use of his two terms, an echo of the different instabilities in 'Tradition and the Individual Talent' as a whole? If there is such a thing, it will be one of *relation*; and, the subject being *personality*, it will have implications for Eliot himself, at the roots of his own criticism. Unamuno's voice is at the opposite extreme from Eliot's: 'to ask a man about his I is like asking him about his body. And note that in speaking of the I, I speak of the concrete and personal I'.[9] There is no need here to ask whether such a conception of personality is 'philosophically justified': it exists, and can be used as a measure of Eliot's own attitude. It is inevitable that it will be. And there are even, in fact, as we shall see, frequent moments when Eliot speaks in the same way; confidently *for* the virtues of personality, without the ambiguousness of his remark in 'Tradition' that 'only those who have personality ... know what it means to want to escape from [it]'. We do not quite know, there, what value to give the word. On those occasions when Eliot speaks for personality-self, however much the firmness contributes to the overall paradoxicality of his position, at least he can not run himself into the kind of difficulty noted by Stephen Spender: 'an escape from personality which is an escape from emotion *is* an expression of personality'.[10]

To sift through Eliot's uses of the word *personal* in his critical and social-critical writings is to discover a surprising consistency—

or persistence—of interest in the topic and, in the expression of that interest, some of the finest passages in the essays. Indeed, in the light of some of these, Eliot's more negative remarks and statements (as in the passage quoted above, or in the remark about the need for 'continual extinction') can suddenly flash another side: in the word 'continual' itself, perhaps, we can see the persistence of the personality's will-to-be against another, more intellectual determination. And likewise, the phrase 'it is only those who have personality and emotions' contains the implicit vaunt that these are things to prize, and Eliot possesses them. If we think that our sense of ourselves as a person, as an identity, is inseparable from our sense of ourself as a personality (we find it hard to separate the words clearly), then ridding oneself of the last item could amount to much more than the expulsion of a bad habit. Extinction means just that, whatever one is doing: it cannot mean that the intention is to bring the quality into a proper (that is, stable and whole) relation with other qualities. This would be true even if we were to take *personality* only in the special sense that Eliot tries to give it, associated with the ' "opinion" and "rhetoric" which he, in common with Yeats, felt had marred poetry in the mid-nineteenth century'[11]—for those terms too can be given positive as well as negative charges of 'value'. What, for example, of the presence in Shakespeare and Jonson of Quintilian's rhetoric as it was transmitted through Ramus?[12] And we all have opinions—we would not be selves unless we had. If there is something wrong with these things it is because their relation with other elements has been disturbed: some centre will not hold, the consort of qualities that makes up a social or personality 'universe' isn't dancing together, and single elements become exorbitant. Consequently opinions became accursed, rhetoric belongs only to politicians, and personality assimilates to egotism. Eliot's criticism exists in the midst of such distortions. Although he tries to correct them, he is still affected by them—the word personality ends up with both a positive and a negative charge at the same moment in a single use and the context does not properly limit the meaning. As we read, we are unsettled: it is rather like looking at the perceptual diagram again—except that we can see the face and the vase at once when we should only see the one or the other. That is a perceptual, then a psychological, then a moral, then an 'aesthetic' law. The 'principle of unity' is to *be*: one thing and not another thing. And one analogy for unity of personality is the unity of the poem: in Milton's words, again: 'oneself the true poem'.

POSITIVE AND NEGATIVE 'PERSONALITY'

If we find Eliot in 'Tradition and the Individual Talent' thinking of personality-impersonality in a way that involves analytic separations, divisions and splits leading into ambiguity, things can be quite different elsewhere. He can imply unity, connection, the inextricability of one thing from another: *relation*, as here:

> the development of genuine taste, founded on genuine feeling, is inextricable from the development of personality and character. Genuine taste is always imperfect taste—but we are all, as a matter of fact, imperfect people; and the man whose taste in poetry does not bear the stamp of his particular personality, so that there are differences in what he likes from what we like as well as resemblances, and differences in the way of liking the same things, is apt to be a very uninteresting person with whom to discuss poetry.[13]

This is as positive a use of the word as one will find in Eliot's critical writing: not something one would wish to 'escape from', if one could. For it appears here that Eliot sees personality as identity, co-terminous with the self; to be without it would be to be badly wanting. It is an example of a not-uncharacteristic assertiveness on Eliot's part; but no less characteristic is the footnote he adds to the first sentence above:

> In making this statement I refuse to be drawn into any discussion of the definition of 'personality' and 'character'.[14]

This is blunt enough, but it hardly expresses confidence—it is the bluster of an insecurity, a reflex brusqueness of dismissal when nothing has been said in contradiction. The footnote neither does any work for Eliot, nor can it possibly stop discussion. It would even be taken as an invitation to harassment. The meanings of the words in the first passage are perfectly clear: they are our ordinary uses. What kind of 'definition', then, could improve

6

on those given by the context? Only, presumably, something 'scientific'. And why, particularly, worry about those words—why not 'taste', or 'genuine'? Any word is open to eristic attack. Of course, Eliot has psychologizing members of the audience in mind (the essays were first given as lectures in America)—but this would not be the way to get them to sit down. Only a real argument, where Eliot was sure of his ground, could do that. We suspect consequently that these are words to which Eliot is peculiarly sensitive, remembering, perhaps, what he had said in 'Tradition and the Individual Talent' some sixteen years before. The two uses aren't in line, and he makes no attempt to bring them into such a relation. Moreover, there are other marks of an uneasiness about the critical discontinuity of the two essays. For in the preface to the 1964 edition of *The Use of Poetry and the Use of Criticism* we find (along with the well-I-don't-knowing over 'La Figlia Che Piange') a description of 'Tradition' as 'perhaps the most juvenile' of his essays. This is combined with the 'faint hope' that a future anthologist will choose one of the lectures to represent his criticism, and is followed by the remark that his 'earliest critical essays . . . came to seem, to him 'the product of immaturity', although: 'I do not repudiate "Tradition and the Individual Talent".'—What will Eliot stand up for clearly, without wanting to take it away again; and without wanting to take back his taking-away? Where is the personal 'principle of unity and continuity' of Unamuno? Has one, at best, to speak of Eliot as consistent in his inconsistency?

It will not do, perhaps, to place too much weight on the skirmishes of prefaces, or the bluffness of a footnote—a sudden failure of nerve before one's own outspokenness.[15] But the almost-baffling shifts in the meaning of the word *personality* in the opening paragraph of the 1927 essay on Thomas Middleton does suggest that something deeper lies behind the discontinuities: on the one hand an intense preoccupation; on the other hand a withdrawal from the necessary confronting of the preoccupation:

It is difficult to imagine his [Middleton's] 'personality'. Several new personalities have recently been fitted to the name of Shakespeare; Jonson is a real figure—our imagination plays about him discoursing at the Mermaid, or laying down the law to Drummond of Hawthornden; Chapman has become a breezy British character as firm as Nelson or Wellington; Webster and Donne are real people for the more intellectual; even Tourneur ... is a 'personality'. But Middleton, who collaborated shamelessly, who is hardly separated from Rowley, Middleton who wrote plays so diverse as *Women Beware Women* and *A Game at Chess* and *The Roaring Girl*, Middleton remains merely a collaborative name for a number of plays— some of which ... are patently by other people.

If we write about Middleton's plays we must write about Middleton's plays and not about Middleton's personality ...[16]

When we come to this knowing that Eliot has a special interest in, and meaning for (and a special dislike for certain meanings of) this term, we find ourselves disconcerted. He *is*, in a way, writing about personality. To adapt Spender's remark: an escape from personality which entails talking about personality as much as Eliot does is an expression of personality. And what of the passage as 'rhetoric'; a journalistic-academic rhetoric written with an eye on a particular audience—'appreciative'. Eliot only half-imports his own standards—elsewhere quite clearly declared—into his own expression. Consequently he winds himself up into paradoxes. And if we are to answer this charge by remarking that we are all capable of it, still something is left to criticize. Eliot, the style tells us, is playing with something of deep personal interest to him. Elsewhere in the essay (and in the middle of this passage) his more settled intention appears, whereas here the word personality flickers between the positive and the negative charge—the inverted commas come and go and return inconsistently: 'a breezy British character' with its critically-placing tone, shifts too easily into 'real people' and the word *real* here is different again from its earlier application to Jonson. Does the disappearance of inverted commas at the end mean something? Does the word 'must' there signify that we can't help but read Middleton in the 'purer' way, or is it injunctive—a sucker growing from the remark that we should focus on the poetry and not the poet? The answer is presumably that both meanings are present; but *we ought to do this* and *we can't do differently*, duty and helplessness, don't go easily together. The meaning refracts—and so it does from *personality*.

'Firm', 'real', 'superficial', 'false' (?), 'bluffly apparent' are all
there. The ground shifts and yet, suddenly, we are presented with
the justly-famous remark ('Middleton remains merely the collec-
tive name for a number of plays')[17] that has made criticism think
differently about Middleton ever since, as we have had to think
anew about Marvell, Donne, 'sensibility' or 'thought' since
Eliot's remarks on them. And yet—yet again—isn't there a simple
mystification here, also? We just don't happen to know anything
about Middleton, and that is all we know (perhaps to our relief).[18]
What should we make of that? As much as Eliot does? The hill is
not particularly cragged or steep, but still the reader about must,
and about must, go.

To look for so long as we have done at a passage such as this is
to have one's confidence in words unsettled, admittedly. What
would stand up to it? Is it fair? But what we see here is of a piece
with what is within the essays as a whole. To say that it is 'just'
one of the effects of writing occasional journalism may be an
explanation but not necessarily an excuse. And would one not
expect the search for settled judgment to return to the subject in
some way throughout years of re-publication, to have tried to get
the matter right as one might get a poem 'right'? We don't expect
such things in criticism. The conclusion seems likely that it was
something that Eliot was unable to settle with himself. Eight years
after 'Tradition', the word *personality* has not subsided into a
steady and habitual use. It surely takes a particular man in particular circumstances for this to happen. And Eliot is a man from
whom we still derive our highest standards.

We should also notice that two sentences after the passage
quoted above Eliot goes on:

> Of all the Elizabethan dramatists Middleton seems the most
> impersonal, the most indifferent to personal fame or perpetuity,
> the readiest, except Rowley, to accept collaboration.[19]

Impersonal here points us to the idea of tradition once again; but
its meanings go in more than the one direction: backwards to
what Eliot has just said; inwards to the nature of the man Middleton; and outwards to the externals of fame. One might want the
latter and still stay, in another sense, impersonal. Part of Eliot's
difficulty lies, of course, in the nature of the words; slippery terms

that it becomes even harder to hold on to at a certain point in history. One *can* say: 'we know what he means'. But if we do we 'see through' what he says, rather than have the meaning clearly presented.

Eliot's *persistence* of interest in the topic is not, in short, *consistent*. For that, his terms would have to be used with a continuity of *personal* meaning sufficiently enforced throughout the essays. In the earlier passage the possibility of that happening is interfered with by playing with the dictionary meanings, or rather, and to be semantically strict, by shifting about between the terms of a definition which is still not a *use*. Eliot's own intention is withdrawn. It is not, to put it in another way, that Eliot is being too much the poet here, but too little. The essential element of his 'I' has gone into something like the ventriloquisms that make up so much of the second part of 'Tradition'. He does not, *here*, face the personal-poetic interest he has in impersonality and personality.

There cannot be any doubt of the depth of that interest. It comes in continual outcrops of curiously short-winded (that too has its significance) but startlingly plain enunciations, from the earliest criticism to the later. If 'Tradition' is the most sustained attempt to express the relation between poem and poet, with its emphasis on the extinction of self before the burden, many other remarks reinforce our sense of the positive value of personality for him, and make the comment about 'wanting to escape' sound more plaintive:

(a) Marlowe's and Jonson's comedies were a view of life; they were, as great literature is, the transformation of a personality into a work of art, their lifetime's work, long or short. Massinger is not simply a smaller personality, his personality hardly exists. He did not, out of his own personality, build a work of art . . .[20]

(b) The creation of a work of art, we will say the creation of a character in a drama, consists in the process of transfusion of the personality, or, in a deeper sense, the life, of the author into the character.[21]

(c) . . . it is not, in the end, periods and traditions but individual men who write great prose . . . The Arts require that a man be not a member of a caste or a party or of a coterie, but

simply and solely himself . . . there is only one man better
and more uncommon than the patrician, and that is the
individual.[22]

(d) What may be considered corrupt or decadent in the morals
of Massinger is not an alteration or diminution in morals;
it is simply the disappearance of all the personal and real
emotions which this morality supported and into which it
introduced a kind of order. As soon as the emotions disappear the morality which ordered it appears hideous.[23]

(e) Had Massinger been a greater man, a man of more intellectual courage, the current of English Literature might
have taken a different course. The defect is precisely a defect
of personality.[24]

Some of these things might almost have been said by the author
we have taken as one measure of difference from 'Tradition':
Unamuno. *Personality* lies firmly in context with the individual,
the self, the 'real', the man—in short, with identity understood as
a wholeness achieving full expression through and in art (it is
'transfused into' the play or poem). And it appears from (d) that
the man-poet and the world-experience, self and morality, are at
one in the genuine work of art. There is no splitting-off, no
separation. They are both personal and impersonal *at one and the
same time*. The poem or play, one might say, is the proof of our
earlier contention that the true 'concept' is not *personal* or *impersonal*, but *personal/impersonal*, with the former logically upper-
most. This is something we can only 'see' in its embodiment: in
man or in poem. It is extremely difficult to express the relation
more fully; but to express it as Eliot has done in these examples
from his earlier criticism (they date from about the same time as
'Tradition') is to say something quite different from this: 'the poet
has not a personality to express but a particular medium, which is
only a medium and not a personality'.[25] How is a medium
expressed? How does it exist? How can we know it without its
expressing something other than itself? A language exists in its
utterances: nowhere else. A medium only exists in relation, as
personal and real emotions exist with morality, above. Tradition
needs the individual talent, as Eliot himself implies in the first part
of that essay; and the need is expressed in that wonderfully reflex-

ive style sustained *like a poem* through those few pages. If all that Eliot 'really means' is that the poet must submit himself to the impersonalizing othernesses of the language, the tradition, conventions or morality, existing prior to, and also in the moment of, writing—the way in which he says it suggests something more like a will to obliteration ('not personality, a medium, *only* a medium') which, to repeat, coexists with the word 'extinction' on another powerful plane of his own personality. Moreover, while the impersonality of Middleton is given a positive value— but it is odd how easily Eliot passes from 'artist' to 'artisan' in 'a great artist or artisan';[26] as if they were synonymous—the criticism of Massinger is that 'his personality hardly exists'. The implication here must be that at some moments in the changing conditions of a society something like a 'lack of character' or identity need not be such a disadvantage; at other times it is; and for Massinger, coming later (though he died in 1640, Middleton only thirteen years earlier) it was. In other words *everything lies in the relation between the self and the society*. But nothing explicit is said of this by Eliot, just as he rarely attempts to express the ideal relation between them.[27] It is odd, if we consider that the persistence of the interest must come from reflection on the relation between himself and his own circumstances. It is *not* just an intellectual or academic interest.

WHOLENESS, ANALYSIS AND KNOWLEDGE

Eliot's view of his world needs to be connected with his failure to settle his discussion of the place of personality in poetry with himself; and something will be offered on that below. At the moment a different connection should be made; between his sense of non-egotistical personality, personality-as-identity (as expressed in parts of 'Tradition and the Individual Talent' and, say, in *Coriolan*) and his very occasional use of the word *whole*. When that word *is* used, it rarely, if ever, refers to the poet, but to the poem—as if that is the only place where Eliot can see the possibility of achieved wholeness. A sad look-out for the rest of us. Occasionally the word *unity* is substituted; a critical term for the moral-psychological. Nevertheless one can detect a fight for wholeness throughout Eliot's criticism; for the 'unity of being' which justifies C. K. Stead's claim that his 'concern for wholeness of sensibility [is] hardly separable from a desire to re-establish a correct relation with the audience for poetry'.[28] But the desire for wholeness takes its force from its very absence, an absence which is something *felt*, personally not 'aesthetically'. The force of the desire is connected with a disability, in the way hinted-at here:

> we have to recognize, I think, that one of the effects of the disability was intensity, and without the intensity . . .—I won't develop that consideration further than to say that the distinctive Eliotic intensity was a necessary condition of that astonishing feat of sustained creative integrity, *Four Quartets*.[29]

The essay on Massinger is again the support for saying that Eliot frequently used the word *personality* to indicate an un-ambiguous and unparadoxical wholeness of being, free from disturbance. The failure of personality in Massinger is described in this way:

> The good poet welds his theft into a whole of feeling which is unique, utterly different from that from which it was torn; the bad poet throws it into something which has no cohesion.[30]

Eliot is clearly thinking of his own borrowing and of what he tried to do with it. But the remark can only imply that the wholes of feeling (poems) issue from wholes of feeling (the man-poet) *or* by deliberated effort out of an inner division—which one feels is more the case with Eliot, and with the twentieth century as less than whole.[31] This genuine integrity is opposed to that of Massinger or Fletcher (and here Eliot might have been thinking of objections to the 'method' of *The Waste Land*) which is a 'synthetic cunning' skilfully welding-together 'parts which have no reason for being together', fabricating plays 'so well knit and so remote from unity'; a unity which, in a living dramatic character, is an 'emotional unity'.[32]

But, wholeness being wholeness (the idea-term is an absolute and can't be subdivided, unless we use it scientifically or quanti-tively to mean the sum of the analysed parts, a meaning which Eliot could not allow himself here) it is not clear why the unity should be *emotional*, particularly when we consider a further con-nected expression of this insistent preoccupation which appears in his essays on the Metaphysicals and on Marvell and again in the important, and rather neglected, essay on Massinger. The unity applauded there is one of intellect and feeling ('blood, intellect and imagination running together', in W. B. Yeats' words):[33] the period before Massinger was one where the 'intellect was immediately at the tips of the senses', where there was, 'a quality of sensuous thought, or of thinking through the senses, or of the senses thinking, of which the exact formula remains to be defined.'[34] (That it could be *defined*, especially by a 'formula'; or that it could be better put than it is in various places by Eliot himself is a separate puzzle. Eliot's language moves so unconsciously towards the very things he speaks against; we have a momentary recapitulation of part II of 'Tradition'; the language of the very analysis that Massinger's style prefigures.) And there are other statements of this principle in such places as the essay on Marvell, where wit is 'this modest and certainly impersonal virtue'; and in the essay on the Metaphysicals, where 'a thought to Donne was an experience: it modified his sensibility' and where 'in the mind of the poet [different kinds] of experience are always forming new wholes.'[35]

Wholeness *is* wholeness. Although it may be affirmed once again that these things would not have been said at all (let alone with such sharpness) without the awareness of division in self and society which Eliot possessed and suffered from and set himself to heal: it must still be said (it is an extension of the paradox) that only such a self in such a society could think of trying to 'define' such a matter in 'exact formula'. The 'technique' of definition, directly related to the 'method' of classification, precisely involves separation, or division, into *genera* and *differentia*. Philosophic definition since Aristotle was mediated through Bacon[36] has been part of the scientific-analytic way of looking at the world; and *definition*, as the word is repeatedly used in Eliot's criticism (see 'Tradition and the Individual Talent' in particular) is never 'placed' in a way that shows that Eliot is properly conscious of these affiliations. It is as if he could not quite see that there might be in that scientific-analytic frame of mind a contributory cause of the divisions he wished to heal. The reader's repeated sense that things that should be connected are not *quite*, is strengthened by Eliot's not-infrequent references to the splitting-up of temperament

since the 'Shakespearean moment'. There is an odd occlusion
in Eliot's thought which allows him to say things like this:

> When a distinguished critic observed recently, in a newspaper
> article, that 'poetry is the most highly organized form of intel-
> lectual activity', we were conscious that we were reading neither
> Coleridge nor Arnold. Not only have the words 'organized'
> and 'activity' . . . that familiar vague suggestion of the scientific
> vocabulary which is characteristic of modern writing, but one
> asked questions which Coleridge and Arnold would not have
> permitted one to ask . . . if a phrase like 'the most highly
> organized form of intellectual activity' is the highest organiza-
> tion of thought of which contemporary criticism is capable,
> then, we conclude, modern criticism is degenerate.
>
> The verbal disease above noticed may be reserved for diag-
> nosis by-and-by . . .[37]

The 'disease' is explicitly associated with 'the scientific vocabulary',
even though it—characteristically—is not quite openly *named*. It
must have something to do with the effects of scientific habits—of
science *as a habit*. Eliot disapproves—'degenerate' proposes a
diagnosis—and yet will make use of (and most notoriously in his
most famous essay) that vocabulary himself.[38] In the very same
essay these phrases occur: 'to analyse and construct', to '*ériger en
lois*' (it is never quite settled whether the word *lois* is the scientific
or legal metaphor), 'some writers are essentially of the type that
reacts in excess of the stimulus' (p. 6). And when Eliot considers
Dryden's criticism (p. 12) he says that:

> There is always a tendency to legislate rather than enquire, to
> revise accepted laws, even to overturn, but to reconstruct out
> of the same material. And the free intelligence is wholly devoted
> to inquiry.[39]

This does not look as though 'loi' is legal 'law', but more of an
analogy with the scientific. 'Ériger en lois ses impressions perso-
nelles, c'est le grand effort d'un homme s'il est sincère'—the
famous dictum Eliot found in de Gourmont stands at the head of
the essay implying an effort towards a settled judgment of *either*
a legal *or* a scientific 'model'; of Dryden's or of Johnson's kind;
or Galileo's. The last sentence above does not however quite

match with this. It could, easily enough, if the task of *ériger en lois*
were seen as a continuous reciprocation of correction and modi-
fication. But Eliot's statement sees them as disconnected, and it
becomes too easy to read 'enquiry' as the endless asking of questions without result, and 'free' as meaning 'loose' or 'ungrounded'
by any deeper aim.[40] We know that such an interpretation would
not tally with Eliot's achievement as a whole, nor with other
expressed opinions of his; but the point is that here (and it happens
again and again) he does not press things into a proper connected-
ness, and this failure is linked with the fact that 'The Perfect
Critic' is itself tinged with a scientific-philosophic habit of thought
and language. There is an indubitable contradiction here. Eliot is
existing in two camps *at once*, and the one interferes with the other.
The elements of his time which are in Eliot (and of course they
are 'in' everyone at any one time), and which he himself says he
dislikes, at the same moment prevent him from freeing himself:
the liberating religious impulse which came later[41] worked itself
into the poetry. At this stage, when Eliot tries to free himself the
effort results in:

> Aristotle had what is called the scientific mind—a mind which,
> as it is rarely found among scientists except in fragments, might
> better be called the intelligent mind. For there is no other
> intelligence than this, and so far as artists and men of letters are
> intelligent, their intelligence is of this kind.[42]

The impulse here is in a way admirable—the assertion of a
general intelligence; but it collapses the distinctions which we all
need (between science, philosophy, criticism and poetry) and
which most readily exist as distinctions and in harmony within
an overall view of the world for which we will need the word
religious. One has in mind here such a wholesale criticism of
modern science as is offered by the Jewish-Christian mystic
Simone Weil (whom Eliot admired)[43] for whom positivist
science was not 'real' science at all.[44] That was represented by
Greek science which existed within an encompassing religious-
poetic world-view. (It is very significant that here Eliot doesn't
ask himself whether Aristotle's 'scientific mind' was essentially
different from the positivist mind.) Eliot, even after his conversion
still lived within the positivist world in a way that Simone Weil

did not: for her it was always The Great Beast, for Eliot it was so only occasionally; though he very frequently implies that the effects of the scientific mind have not, for the unified sensibility, and therefore for the possibility of poetry, been all good:

> The vast accumulations of knowledge—or at least of informa-
> tion—deposited by the nineteenth century have been respon-
> sible for an equally vast ignorance. When there is so much to
> be known, when there are so many fields of knowledge in
> which the same words are used with different meanings, when
> everyone knows a little about a great many things, it becomes
> increasingly difficult for anyone to know whether he knows
> what he is talking about or not.[45]

The personal note here tells us that Eliot is aware that this is the predicament in which he writes, and that he knows, as Tennyson knew (*Gerontion* follows *Ulysses*) that the vast accumulation is the direct result of the spread of scientific enquiry. He doesn't quite say, however, that more is at issue than a matter of quantity: an absence of shape, or meaning. And without that settled sense, which is a settled conviction, Eliot's own meanings waver. He both fights against and too much reflects his times. He knows what, as a poet and man, he needs—'unity of being'; he knows that his needs are threatened; he knows the source of the threat ... and yet, between his knowledge and the response there is a shadow. Remembering the ending of 'The Hollow Men' one would not dare to suggest that Eliot did not know that too, in the deepest conflicts of his personality.

THE 'MANIFEST FISSURE'

A thorough reading of Eliot's criticism cannot leave one with any doubt that he did suspect—but 'suspect' is even too definite a word—that scientific enquiry and its consequences were the chief source of that 'dissociation of sensibility' he saw his own age (and if his suspicions had been stronger he would have to implicate himself in the age) as suffering from. The phrase itself of course comes from the 1921 essay on 'The Metaphysical Poets', where it is described as a 'theory' (though it is hardly that, being no more extensive than the remarks on the 'objective correlative')[46] and where again the language in which the 'theory' is expressed has the same scientific-mechanistic tinge:

> The poets of the seventeenth century, the successors of the dramatists of the sixteenth, possessed a mechanism of sensibility which could devour any kind of experience ... In the seventeenth century a dissociation of sensibility set in, from which we have never recovered; and this dissociation, as is natural, was aggravated by the influence of the two most powerful poets of the century ... (etc.)[47]

Eliot adds that in the eighteenth century, then in the nineteenth

> the poets revolted against the ratiocinative, the descriptive; they thought and felt by fits, unbalanced ... In one or two passages of Shelley's *Triumph of Life*, in the second *Hyperion*, there are traces of a struggle towards unification of sensibility ...[48]

This 'theory' is continuous with the persistent interest in wholeness—'unification'—and of a piece with numerous other scattered remarks, embodied in memorable metaphor, of the 'intellect at the tips of the senses' kind. (It is interesting to note the affinity here with the concentration of sensation in image in Yeats' remark that in looking at a Canaletto 'our thought rushes to the edges of our flesh'.) And we can 'put together' a historical theory out of these scattered remarks—one reaching, as we shall shortly see, into the future. And once we have assembled it, it is 'consistent'; in the scatterings of remarks, both pregnant and pointed, that Eliot does not finally *ériger en lois*: they achieve that curious status, fascinating to so many critics, of hovering between a clear impersonalized enunciation, and being passing, and personal, 'remarks'. The remarks constantly *imply*; and in this, they are themselves rather like metaphors, seeming to husband some of their meaning as it were for future use. But a *historical* meaning is present, and one could almost make a simple graph of it—the decline of one kind of sensibility against another. And it is in the terms of the rise of the latter ('ratiocinative, descriptive' above) that we ask Eliot for more 'evidence', more 'reasons': the extrapolated *case*. This, too, involves a paradox, for it means that we, the ratiocinative academic critics, are taking Eliot in a way which he frequently seems to repudiate: Henry James, Eliot remarked in 1918, had 'a mind so fine that no idea could violate it'. In the full context, this has a wider bearing than the touch of aestheticism in it might at first suggest. Eliot himself is in the difficulty that we are in, if he takes his own remarks about Aristotle and the scientific mind seriously—pulled one way by the ratiocinative, the other way by the anti-ratiocinative. And yet, his very sense of the difficulty gives his remarks their *personal* force. He doesn't 'raise personal impressions into [explicit] laws'; he tends to hover between the insight and its completion, and it was left to others— for example L. C. Knights in 'Bacon and the Seventeenth Century Dissociation of Sensibility'[49] to try to provide the latter, to establish the connections, as Knights remarks, without 'any kind of anti-scientific hocus-pocus', adding that,

> What we need is not to abandon reason, but simply to recognize that reason in the last three centuries has worked within a field which is not the whole of experience, that it has mistaken the part for the whole . . . there are still gains to be won by reason.[50]

The 'new Criticism' followed from Eliot: his personal insights, those of poet and man, needed the extension and 'rationalization' they received. Eliot himself never quite did what the canons of '*loi*' require, construct something like a statement out of his intuitions—too many contradictions are present for us to feel that that was a possibility. It is, for example, an odd characteristic of his criticism, which I have already noted, that he had relatively so little to say of Shakespeare—that he did not read back into his criticism (so that it would have permeated the whole) the example presented by *that* unified sensibility. Or one might add that he has even less to say of Chaucer.[51] He turned, instead to Dante, in two of his finest essays:[52] to a poet in whom dogma is more *apparent*, a 'philosophy' surpassingly, but still plainly, 'in' the poetry. Connected with this too is the intense early approbation of the Metaphysicals. It was not until 1931[53] that Eliot wrote of Donne that in him 'there is a manifest fissure of thought and sensibility'. Previously, he had defended the Metaphysicals against Johnson's charge that 'the most heterogeneous ideas are yoked by violence together' by saying that 'after the dissociation they [the Metaphysicals] put the material together into a new unity',[54] and by claiming by implication that Donne's mind was 'perfectly equipped for its work'. If he had not noticed the fissure so forcibly before—if he saw something else—the reason would in all likelihood have been the intense attraction for him at that time, in his anxious search for unity, of the Metaphysicals. He was in fact seeing the fissure and not recognising its significance; seeing actually *in* them the beginnings of a dissociation of sensibility of thought from feeling, which, however, had not developed so far that Donne and Marvell could not hold the two parts of the divided sensibility together. Eliot, in short, was seeing himself 'in' them, but not fully taking the significance of what he saw for himself. To put it more shortly still: *he doesn't see his own position*:

> In very general terms it might be said that the notion of a pregnant historical crisis ... was attractive because ... it explained in a subtly agreeable way the torment and division of modern life ... Feeling and thinking by turns ... a double-minded period measured itself ...[55]

Similarity, however, can be something of a trap; it need tell us no more about ourselves than difference. The latter is some protection against seeing what we want to see, only.

We feel ourselves encountering here a complex set of cross references between literary history, personality and style; as if the view of history were participating with history itself. Eliot himself participates through style, which is the expression of himself in his own time: history is in fact being re-written, not 'accurately' but according to creative purpose. If Eliot's criticism is described as unhistorical,[56] or mythical, we should remember that it is a very modern usage that makes *myth* synonymous with *lie*. Perhaps the juster criticism would be that the creative reconstruction is not encompassing enough: for that the measure would be, not the Metaphysicals, but: Dante, Shakespeare, Chaucer. At any rate, if Bacon 'points forward to the conscious and unconscious utilitarianism of the nineteenth century, of which we ourselves are the embarrassed heirs'[57], then Eliot's critical essays and their style, are an index of the effects of that emergence, where the sensibility is either divided, or achieves a reduced integrity through an accommodation to a positivist view of the world, or—our greatest hope—reaches to the wholeness that does not, in Knights' words, mistake the part for the whole.

One should do everything possible to avoid giving the impression that Eliot did not 'know' his personal-historical predicament in the deepest sense. It is only that this sense was not raised into a coherent conscious 'position'. The intuitive need was perhaps so great that it would have been violated by rational excogitation. His 'theories' consequently stand out like assertions, and irritate and puzzle many readers. However, these theories, which shade into such things as the remarks on Baudelaire's search for a 'form of life', the central interest in Dante and the relation of 'philosophy' to poetry, the recurring assertion of the need for conventions and the support of morality; these are all essentially the *expressions* of a single pressing interest which appears and re-appears in the frequent comments on his own times, masquerading as mere asides. Here, for example, we have the idea of dissociation expressed in different terms (Eliot is disagreeing with some views of Sir Herbert Read's):

> What I see, in the history of English poetry, is not so much demonic possession as the splitting-up of personality. If we say that one of these partial personalities which may develop in a national mind is that which manifested itself in the period between Dryden and Johnson, then what we have to do is to re-integrate it: otherwise we are likely to get only successive alterations of personality. Surely the great poet is, among other things, one who not merely restores a tradition, but one who in his poetry re-twines as many straying strands of tradition as possible. Nor can you isolate poetry from everything else in the the history of a people; and it is rather strong to suggest that the English mind has been deranged ever since the time of Shakespeare, and that only recently have a few fitful rays of reason penetrated the darkness. If the malady is as chronic as that, it is pretty well beyond cure.[58]

Again the reader has that sense of a strong insight being baffled. We are offered something like a complete view of literary history, and one in keeping with other remarks of Eliot's, and yet the certainty of the statement is towards the end withdrawn. If he does see the history in this way—if the idea of 'dissociation' has

been taken up by Sir Herbert Read—Eliot himself is largely
responsible, and it *is* a bit strong of *him* to object in that way to
Sir Herbert's suggestion of 'derangement'. 'Splitting-up', and
'dissociation' are not so very far away, nor are the ideas of 'split
personality' or, even, schizophrenia.[59] It is to be suspected that
Eliot is fending-off the danger that he himself, having offered his
diagnosis, might be seen as the great poet who restores the tradition; but that decent depreciation is here somewhat at odds with
the tone of the opening. Once again a forceful impulse remains
uncompleted; the reader feels that something has been given, and
then half-taken away.

A further, more obvious example of this occurs in the lecture
'From Poe to Valéry', given in 1948, but not printed in book form
until *To Criticize the Critic* (1965):

> as for the future: it is a tenable hypothesis that this advance of
> self-consciousness, the extreme awareness of and concern for
> language which we find in Valéry, is something which must
> ultimately break down, owing to an increasing strain against
> which the human mind and nerves will rebel; just as, it may be
> maintained, the indefinite elaboration of scientific discovery and
> invention, and of political and social machinery, may reach a
> point at which there will be an irresistible revulsion of humanity
> and a readiness to accept the most primitive hardships rather
> than carry on any longer the burden of modern civilization.
> Upon that I hold no fixed opinion: I leave it to your con-
> sideration.[60]

An urgent expression of anxiety about the condition of his own
culture (containing one of his few direct references in his literary
criticism to the elaboration and fragmentation of knowledge consequent on a science uncontrolled by other cultural meaning) is
undermined by the bureaucratization of his language in the last
sentence. He has just told us quite clearly what he thinks, despite
the 'mays', 'a tenable hypothesis that' and 'it may be maintained'.
We know from *The Waste Land* at least, that modern civilization
was a burden to Eliot himself: 'the nightmare of history'. If the
opinion was not 'fixed', it could by now have been settled; and it
is still far from being the kind of opinion that might be put forward 'for argument's sake'. Its sources are elsewhere, continuous

with the interest in personality and the changes that occur in personality in different cultural circumstances; continuous with his struggle for an impersonality through the medium, language, 'tradition', or orthodoxy. The personal roots seem to lie in his sense of the effects of the modern world upon the person, and particularly the heightened representativeness of the poet:

> We can assert with some confidence that our own period is one of decline; that the standards of culture are lower than they were fifty years ago; and that the evidences of this decline are visible in every department of human activity. I see no reason why the decay of culture should not proceed much further, and why we may not even anticipate a period, of some duration, of which it is possible to say that it will have no culture.[61]

The difficulty is that the expression of the personal concern is constantly being *suppressed*.[62] Though the intention is doubtless to *impersonalize* (even through the adopted manner of the civil servant as of the scientific lecturer in 'Tradition') one can't say that it is achieved. Eliot does not seem to be able to trust himself to speak *from himself* for long without fearing that he is being 'personal' in his own pejorative sense. In his own utterance he generally seems to flinch from bringing the two halves of the personal-impersonal conception into the steady relation that would be required before we could say that either word had a settled meaning. Only occasionally, notably in part I of 'Tradition', the personal impulse unites with the proper wish to generalize in expressions that are among the supreme moments of modern criticism.

NEGATIVE CAPABILITY AND SYSTEMATIC CERTITUDE

Eliot's attempts to explain his sense of the relation between the two terms was not necessarily helped by his philosophical training; the 'linear' nature of ratiocination seems to have been something to which he adapted only with effort; and what he said of Coleridge can be taken again as reflecting his sense of his own case. Richard Wollheim has remarked that:

It would be a subject in itself to study the irony of many of Eliot's pronouncements on literature in general and on his poetry in particular—of which this passage, in which Eliot simultaneously depreciates, and makes clear his own philosophical culture, is a fine example.[63]

Eliot is again giving and taking away. His philosophical culture of course included a training at Harvard, and a thesis, only published late in his life, on the Idealist philosophy of F. H. Bradley.[64] The connections between this work and the 'theory' of personality-impersonality have been traced by Wollheim to the point where,

> there is some ambiguity or uncertainty in Eliot's essays concerning the extent to which the thesis of the impersonality of the poet derives from any philosophical 'disproof' of commonsense notions of personality. Is the 'escape from personality' which is the poetic vocation, a direct logical consequence of the dissolution by Idealism of faulty and ultimately incoherent notions of the self or personality—or is it a mere analogue in critical theory to what in metaphysics is a necessary truth? To put it crudely: Does the poet not express personality because there is no such thing as personality, or because he shouldn't?[65]

Wollheim thinks that the answers to this are not clear, but that there does seem to be a general *tendency* of thought shared by Bradley and Eliot: 'a peculiarly empty or hollow way of conceiving the mind'. The general tendency to ambiguity in Eliot's critical manner (and remembering his characteristically self-deprecating remark that what he mainly drew from Bradley was a prose style)[66] makes one think that what drew him to Bradley was a *personal* interest, not a professional or philosophical one:

> I have written best about writers who have influenced my own poetry. And I say 'writers' and not only 'poets' because I include F. H. Bradley, whose works—I might say whose personality as manifested in his works—affected me profoundly.[67]

and he later speaks of some of his 'theories' as 'conceptual symbols for emotional preferences'.[68] Furthermore he speaks in *The Use of Poetry and the Use of Criticism* of having read 'some of Hegel and Fichte, as well as Hartley (who turns up at any moment with

Coleridge), and forgotten it' and notes of Coleridge's distinction between Fancy and Imagination that his mind 'is too heavy and concrete for any flight of abstruse reasoning'.[69]

There is something in the deprecation to be attended to seriously; we can guess that Eliot is revealing the deeply intuitive nature of his own temperament with which philosophical inquiry would be fundamentally at odds, however much of his life he spent upon it. His nature was essentially the extension of undifferentiated human nature that is a poet's, and specialized rational thought—even perhaps critical thought—compounded rather than healed the divided self for which he desired wholeness. He was able to persist with his thesis for so long (though his degree was never taken) because the conceptual interest *expressed* an 'emotional preference'. The relation of subject to object, of mind to external world, of self to what is other than the self: these were anterior pre-occupations which he found in Bradley, whose attempted equation of the Ideal with the real and consciousness with object[70] pointed towards a wished-for metaphysical reconciliation of inner and outer; a wholeness where Bradley's Immediate Experience 'prefigures the supra-rational unity of the Absolute, in which thought and its object are united to form Truth'.[71] In short, the impulse seems to be one in which the desire for unity of being seeks for a metaphysical justification.

It is difficult to regard both the intensity of the search (focusing itself on the personality-impersonality relation) and the fluctuations of tone and inconsistencies of argument which tend to mask it as anything other than manifestations of the cultural strain he himself recognized, and which may have been aggravated by a matching private circumstance. Private and public reflect one another:

> I only affirm that all human affairs are involved with each other, that consequently all history involves abstraction, and that in attempting to win a full understanding of the poetry of a period you are led to the consideration of subjects which at first sight seem to have little bearing upon poetry.[72]

That might have been taken as a second epigraph to the present essay. Eliot, as we all are, is representative; and in describing himself as 'a minor poet' and in saying that in 'a formless age there is little hope for the minor poet to do anything worth doing'[73] he implies also that with 'too much to do' the human hope of becoming (what we might wish to become) is much reduced.

For Eliot does tend to see society and culture as being 'like' individuals:

> We should look for the improvement of society, as we seek our own individual improvement, in relatively minute particulars. We cannot say: 'I shall make myself into a different person'; we can only say: 'I will give up this or that bad habit, and endeavour to contract this good one.'[74]

Society and individual are continuous: a 'splitting up of personality' in the one would be bound to be reflected in the other. And if Eliot saw the one, he would see, or feel, the other. Even a divided, or non-'unified', world is of a piece in its dividedness. There are signs too here and there in his criticism, that Eliot believed the poetic personality was in his own time particularly vulnerable to the strain. While Wordsworth's genius is described, in a rather reserved way, as having 'something integral about it'[75] (there is perhaps just a touch here of the qualification of Keats' 'egotistical sublime'). Keats' himself is seized upon—it amounts to that—for his remark in the letters that

> Men of Genius are great as certain ethereal chemicals operating on the mass of neutral intellect—but they have not any individuality, and determined character—I would call the top and head of those who have a proper self Men of Power.[76]

This, says Eliot, 'can only be called the result of genius'. It is very hard indeed not to see Eliot's attentiveness towards Keats as an attraction of preoccupations with the nature of poetic personality. But Keats' grasp of the matter is much surer, despite the occasional nature of its expression (letters are a more natural place for fragmentariness). His 'Negative Capability',[77] the term corresponding to Impersonality, is a new invention for something newly perceived—perhaps for the first time with such peculiar Romantic sharpness. The personal jargon is paradoxical in meaning: we have both the positive and the negative charge, *at once*. The positive capacity *is* negative: an openness to experience which obliterates 'personality' (in Eliot's sense), but which is dependent *upon* personality.

What seems to be at issue for both poets is the question of identity and its relation to ego-self. The development of Romanticism and the increased strain of the modern world of which Eliot frequently complained, leading towards a greater isolation of the self, made Eliot a critic of Romanticism, the 'classicist' who spoke for forms, orthodoxies, conventions, moralities.[78] However, there is a subterranean link between the idea of negative capability and that of impersonality, as there is between 'proper self', 'determined character', and 'the man of Power'; and 'personality', 'opinion' ('let her think opinions are accursed'—Yeats' lines too are relevant) and 'rhetoric'—the language of 'men of power', Coriolans. Both Keats and Eliot express a split or division between the character of the poet and the world in which he lives. (The chemical analogy is present in both descriptions too.) This is particularly clear in what Keats has to say of his friend Dilke:

> I wrote Brown a comment on the subject, wherein I explained what I thought of Dilke's character. Which resolved itself into this conclusion. That Dilke was a Man who cannot feel he has a personal identity unless he had made up his mind about everything. The only means of strengthening one's intellect is to make up one's mind about nothing—to let the mind be a thoroughfare for all thoughts . . . All the stubborn arguers you meet with are of the same brood . . . They want to hammer their nail into you and if you turn the point, still they think you wrong. Dilke will never come at a truth as long as he lives; because he is always trying at it. He is a Godwin-methodist.[79]

We are bound think again of Eliot's remark that James had a mind so fine 'that no idea could violate it'—if we stress the word *idea*. And yet, and *yet again*, Eliot's dealings with Keats are still indecisive, and a very small part of his critical work; when one might have felt that his own interest might have suggested to him that here there was something to confront. He moves away with the comment that he is 'not so much concerned with the degree of Keats' greatness as with its kind, and its kind is manifested more clearly in his letters than in his poems'.[80] Eliot's own strangely 'neutral intellect' has a very clear sense of Keats' significance for himself, but it is not excogitated into consciousness and presented to the reader of the criticism. To do so Eliot would have had to present us with *himself* more clearly than he does: as Keats does do.

It is, of course, as much the difference between Eliot and Keats that we wish to note as any similarities. Lionel Trilling has remarked that

> Keats believed that the Negative Capability which made possible the poetic vision of life depended on a personal quality which he thought Dilke lacked ... Negative Capability, the faculty of not having to make up one's mind about everything, *depends upon the sense of one's personal identity and is the sign of personal identity.* Only the self that is certain of its existence, of its identity, can do without the armour of systematic certitude. (My italics.)

Trilling adds in a footnote that

> This is only apparently contradicted by certain notable remarks which Keats made about men of genius in poetry *lacking* personal identity ... in the passages he is speaking of the poet as poet, not of the poet as man.[81]

There is a suggestion here of the way in which impersonality and personality might have been brought together in a clear, though still paradoxical, relation: as we have seen, Eliot's attempts to theorize often resulted in matters moving from the paradoxical into the contradictory. (It is extremely interesting—almost a contradiction of contradictions—to find him saying of Keats that he had 'no theory, and to have formed one was irrelevant to his interests, and alien to his mind'. And again: 'He had no theories, yet in the same sense, though to a lesser degree than Shakespeare, he had a "philosophic" mind.')[82] It is only an actual confidence in identity that allows one to remain in 'uncertainties, Mysteries, doubts, without any irritable searching after fact and reason'.[83] Moreover, a connection is at least assumed between poet and man rather than the separation asserted in 'Tradition and the Individual Talent' ('the more completely separate') by Eliot who nowhere pushes his own interest towards conclusion; just as here, he approaches Keats, and withdraws:

He was occupied only with the highest use of poetry; but that does not imply that poets of other types may not rightly and sometimes by obligation be concerned about the other uses.[84]

To put the matter very bluntly: first, what else is Eliot occupied with? and, second, if he is of the other type (what type of poet *is* it that is not occupied with the highest 'uses' of poetry?) what lesson might he draw for himself? The withdrawal is another example of Eliot's habit of saying his most interesting things in a scattering of fragments, which the very curious reader can reconstruct for himself; and this fragmentation is in turn related to the failure to join personality and impersonality. Disconnected, *neither amounts to identity*: there is a final division between ego-self (the bad sense of personality) and that absence of confident identity which Eliot confronted for himself in 'The Hollow Men'. It is no wonder that he frequently reached for 'the armour of systematic certitude'. It *is* a wonder that the sincerity of creative purpose went far beyond that in the poetry, and therefore beyond any notion of 'use'.

THE EXACTIONS OF SINCERITY

An answer to the inevitable question why Eliot did not make either these distinctions[85] or the necessary conjunctions, has to come in terms whose character will point towards the personal. His tentativeness contrasts with Keats' confidence, a confidence that is necessary for the lack of defensiveness (Dilke's kind of defensiveness) that is genuine openness. Of course, Eliot, in a number of places in both the early and the later criticism, does express the relation between impersonality and personality in ways that it is easy to prefer to some of the *loci classici*. For example:

> I have, in early essays, extolled what I called impersonality in art, and it may seem that, in giving a reason for the superiority of Yeats' later work the greater expression of personality in it, I am contradicting myself. It may be that I expressed myself badly, or that I had only an adolescent grasp of that idea [Eliot elsewhere calls 'Tradition and the Individual Talent' 'juvenile' —he was 32 when it was written.] As I can never bear to re-read

my own prose writing, I am willing to leave the point unsettled [a curious attitude for an important public figure and
poet to take?] but I think now, at least, [words which portend
a future when the matter will remain unsettled, that even what
follows may be retracted] that the matter is as follows. There
are two forms of impersonality: that which is natural to the
mere skilful craftsman, and that which is more and more
achieved by the maturing artist . . . that of the poet who, out
of intense and impersonal experience, is able to express a general
truth; retaining all the particularity of his experience to make
of it a general symbol.[86]

The statement is plain and simple enough to make one wonder
why there is so much preceding fuss. It makes distinctions which
are necessary but which were confused in the essay on Middleton
('artist *or* artisan'), where the underlying idea is similar to that in
an earlier essay:

No artist produces great art by a deliberate attempt to express
his personality. He expresses his personality indirectly through
concentrating on a task in the same sense as the making of an
efficient engine, or the turning of a jug or a table-leg.[87]

The word 'indirectly' suggests possibilities that are not made open
in 'Tradition'—but at the same time we must wonder if the sense
is the same. 'Art' and 'craft' are different words, that point to
activities different in nature. What *is* the difference?

Some critics, for example Smidt,[88] or Allen Austin,[89] use
examples such as these, occurring throughout the criticism, to
show a consistency among apparent inconsistency. But this can
only be done if the inconsistency is taken into account: if we go
beyond saying what Eliot 'really meant' to try to say 'what it *all*
means'—the difference would be something like the difference
between Gestalt and faculty psychology. For the examples above
still show an unsettledness: and if we make a pattern of our pre-
ferred statements from Eliot, we can always find others to put
beside them that we like less, from whatever critical period.

One of the problems in fact, is that once we have found the
established classic, 'Tradition and the Individual Talent', wanting
—there *is* no *locus classicus*. It is hard for us to find our feet, and

we are inclined to grab at things. And all this occurs in the context of the formal presentation of ideas, through the potential impersonality of the lecture or the essay. In contrast the informal medium—'personal'—of Keats' letters offers us fragments; but fragments each of which is consistent with the other. Keats' conception is settled (this does not mean of course that we have to 'agree with it') and expresses something that Eliot's impersonality cannot: a positive and self-sustaining impulse in poise with an un-inhibited receptiveness. The ego-self is not standing in the way. It could not be expressed without the confidence to express it, which in turn was continuous with the general Romantic confidence, of feeling 'at home' in the world. (Though here Eliot is probably right in his suggestion that this was one of those 'alternations of personality'[90] which were, in the long run, expressions of the dividing sensibility: separations of self from society.) Still, in contrast to the Romantic expressions of personality, Eliot's own position imposed a defensiveness which in turn made its own exactions.

One warrant for saying so lies in the way in which Eliot speaks of Arnold; linking Arnold with *his* times, drawing both men together:

> I feel, rather than observe, an inner uncertainty and lack of conviction in Matthew Arnold: the conservatism that springs from lack of faith, and the zeal for reform which springs from dislike of change. Perhaps, looking inward and finding *how little he had to support him*, looking outward on the state of society and its tendencies, he was somewhat disturbed. He had no real serenity, only an impeccable demeanour. Perhaps he cared too much for civilization, forgetting that Heaven and Earth shall pass away, and Mr Arnold with them, and there is only one stay. He is a representative figure. A man's theory of the place of poetry is not independent of his view of life in general.[91] (My italics.)

It is hard not to see some of this, at least, as a discharge on to Arnold of more personal thoughts. Yet at the same time there is an uneasiness in the tone which inevitably recalls that hauteur we noted in some of the phrases from 'Tradition and the Individual Talent'. Eliot is, as it were, too close to Arnold (his great predecessor) for him to take this tone. His own conservatism, his own social criticism (particularly *Notes towards the Definition of Culture*) his own disturbed view of the tendencies of the world (of which we have seen several examples), his own lack of serenity associated with a demeanour which (as we can see from Neville Braybrooke's collection of memoirs)[92] was not quite impeccable (whose 'demeanour' could be? what serenity does he expect?) either in the style of his essays or in social life . . . all this brings him too close to Arnold to allow for the tone of 'forgetting that Heaven and Earth shall pass away'. Few could say such things. The very uneasiness of the remarks *is* our warrant for saying that he is more like Arnold than he pretends; but will *not* finally, openly, implicate himself (though the italicized words may make us feel some sympathy). He tries to be superior; and he says that Arnold is a 'representative figure' in a way that suggests he himself is not. Everyone is: we all may have our 'case-histories'.[93] There is here, as there is not in the poetry, a failure to find a 'technique for sincerity'.[94]

Eliot's theories are representative, and representative in a personal way. Impersonality, dissociation of sensibility, the objective correlative: these adjuncts to his modern classicism are of course expressions of the man in his time: and finally they are failures of nerve before the exactions of sincerity. Speaking of the modern devaluation of 'sincerity' (Eliot's struggle for it in his poetry deserves the word heroic) Lionel Trilling has remarked that it is

> bound up in an essential though paradoxical way with the mystique of the classic literature of our century, some of whose masters took the position that, in relation to their work and their audience, they were not persons or selves, they were artists, by which they meant that they were exactly not, in the phrase with which Wordsworth began his definition of the poet, men speaking to men . . .[95]

The appeal to this distinction between the poet and the man is made repeatedly in Eliot's criticism. In this he is at one with the criticism of his time—with Joyce's (or more exactly Stephen Dedalus') statement in chapter five of *Portrait of the Artist as a Young Man*, that 'the personality of the artist finally refines itself out of existence, impersonalizes itself, so to speak'; with Gide's remark that 'the aesthetic point of view is the only sound one to take in discussing my work'; with Hulme's wish for 'a dry hardness', 'a form of objectivism which insists on *clear distinctions* between ethical and religious doctrine and poetic composition'. (The 'clear distinctions' that Hulme, with his technical training, asked for in *Speculations*, were really of the same kind that obtain in, are necessary to, analytic enquiry.)[96]

This 'classical and objective version of organicity'[97] is in fact representative of its time in being deeply affected by, and taking as an undeclared or half-conscious measure what those times assumed science was. Since the work of Kuhn, Polanyi, Marjorie Grene and Laing we think differently of it, and any criticism that is aware of the change will be in turn representative in a different way—differently implicated. Eliot's impersonality, in so far as it reflects a particular view of science, tends not so much towards 'irresponsibility' (Yvor Winters' word) as towards the desire for the relief that the autonomy of a method can give—'the armour of systematic certitude'; of *theory*.

For the application of the last sentence of Eliot's comments about Arnold is inescapable: any man is representative. A man's 'theory' of poetry is not independent of his view of life in general. His view of life in general cannot be independent of the life of his times. He himself is not independent of his times: our minds swim about in them as fish in water. His poetry is not independent of them. Impersonality and personality are not independent of one another. We cannot be free of connection, though we talk, today particularly, as if 'objectivity' (with the 'theories' that go with it) would exempt us. Classic or romantic, form and content, personal and impersonal, are not independent of one another, though they are certainly not 'the same thing'. We can't have an idea of one without the other—the analytic separation that is involved in trying to 'define' singly *is* a dissociation of the sensibility. And if we do think that things only exist in *interrelation*, then the attempt to explain relation is an *active* business and the business of that kind of criticism a *living* business. Such an attempt occurs in the first part of 'Tradition and the Individual Talent': the syntax there was active, flexuose. In it personal and impersonal are *related*, in the English language, which is itself impersonal. The manner is the manner of a poem. As Eliot himself says:

The meaning of a word is at a point of intersection: it arises from its relation first to the words immediately preceding and following it and *indefinitely* to the rest of its context; and from another relation, that of the immediate meaning in that context to all the other meanings that it has in other contexts, to its greater or less wealth of association.[98] (My italics.)

Such a complex combination of relations in meaning and 'music' when it occurs *is* that moment of wholeness or fullness: impersonal. The attempt to 'define' in the second part of 'Tradition' is contrary to the spirit of the word 'indefinitely' above. It is telling that the phrase 'point of intersection' which also occurs above occurs in *Four Quartets*, to express those moments of completeness where the timeless and the temporal join:

> But to apprehend
> The point of intersection of the timeless
> With time,[99]

and again:

> Here, the intersection of the timeless moment
> Is England and nowhere. Never and always.[100]

It would have been quite characteristic of Eliot to know what kind of hint he was dropping in using that particular word. We are left with matters to be followed-up, and the awareness of connections on Eliot's part did not entail, for him, public self-exposure or self-scrutiny. The hint, or fragment, seems to have been particularly congenial to him, as the *consistent* critical effort wasn't: it was not, of course, his primary 'job'. His one attempt at a statement of personality-impersonality resulted, as we have seen, in an actual disconnection between the desire for continuity and the desire to escape from the effort towards conclusiveness. The general impression is of ineradicable paradox, where the interrelatedness of self and what is not of the self is never clearly enough seen to be plainly, openly, stated, as it is by Keats in whom the capability of identity is *for* unegotistical open-ness. The 'negative' is the ally of a positive purpose; the impersonality is integral to the personality; active and passive aren't distinguishable; the 'concept' is *personality-impersonality*. Keats' understanding can only have come from an

instinctive confidence. The source of Eliot's best insights, as well
as of his failures, was a single source, but not one that gave him a
secure confidence. The extraordinary feat of style that is part I of
'Tradition', we feel is just that—a feat, provisional yet final, *like*
a poem.

Paradox begets paradox. Once inside, it is hard to get out. But
finally one is enclosed, and trapped:

> For all their intention of impersonality, they [the practitioners
> of the classic literature of our century] figure in our minds
> exactly as persons, as personalities, of a large exemplary kind,
> asking, each one of them, what his own self is, and whether or
> not he is being true to it, drawing us to emulation of their
> self-scrutiny.[101]

Eliot's self-scrutiny never invited direct questions—in fact the
reverse;[102] but for all that he *is* exemplary, in his perpetual
inclination towards disguise, requests for privacy, insistence on
the separation of poet from man; in his fragmentary utterances
on the subject of self. The enclosing paradox, of course, is that in
our temptation to hide we reveal. We cannot escape from that.
From the consequent tortuousness attendant upon the temptation
the only escape is by the shortest way: straight out.

NOTE A

The Reference to Science:
Metaphor and Dissociation

I add here a very few examples, casually collected from Eliot's
prose, to sketch the way in which (despite his remarks at the
beginning of 'The Perfect Critic') his own vocabulary makes continual reference to science, often through metaphor, and often
implying a curious 'objectivity'. I follow the examples from Eliot
with one or two from other critics.

(a) 'It is *exactly* as wasteful for a poet to do what has been done
already, as for a biologist to re-discover Mendel's discoveries.
The French poets in question have made "discoveries" in verse of

which he cannot afford to be ignorant. To remain with Wordsworth is *equivalent* to ignoring the whole of the science subsequent
to Erasmus Darwin.' (My italics: how exact? How equivalent?)
Quoted in N. H. Pearson and W. R. Benét, *The Oxford Anthology
of American Literature* (New York, Oxford University Press, 1939),
p. 1636.

(b) 'More important than the lack of balance is the lack of
detailed *analysis* . . . Wyndham misses the cardinal point in
criticizing the Elizabethans: we cannot grasp them . . . without
some understanding of the *pathology* of rhetoric [which] was
endemic, it pervaded the whole *organism*; the *healthy* as well as the
morbid tissues were built up on it . . . [we must] *diagnose* the
rhetoric' (*The Sacred Wood*, pp. 30-1).

(c) '[Charles Whibley] exercises neither of the *tools* of the
critic' (*SW* 37).

(d) 'Swinburne's essays would have been all the better if he had
applied himself to *the solution of problems*' (*SW* 23).

(e) 'There are two ways in which a writer may lead us to profit
by the work of dead writers. One is by *isolating* the essential, by
pointing out the most intense in various kinds and *separating* it
from the accidents of the environment. This *method* . . . The
other *method* . . .' (*SW* 28).

The *method* in Eliot's mind here is plainly scientific, where
analysis does involve separating one thing from another. It is
therefore interesting that Eliot frequently praises the critic who
keeps things distinct, who *isolates*: 'the critic needs to be able to
saturate himself in the spirit of a time—the local flavour—but also
to separate himself suddenly from it in appreciation of the highest
creative work' (*SW* 37). To *separate* from *saturation? Suddenly?*
Furthermore: 'Leonardo turned to art or science, and each was
what it was and not another thing' (*SW* 27). Eliot seems to see no
possible danger for personality in analytic separation. Consequently it is only half a surprise, despite the contradiction between what he says here and what he says later about dissociation
of sensibility to find that Charles Whibley is *criticized* for having
'no dissociative faculty' (*SW* 37).

(f) 'The pure moralist in letters must be more *concise*, for we
must have the pleasure of *inspecting* the beauty of his structure'
(*SW* 41).

(g) Julien Benda is praised for 'manipulating' ideas; but on the other hand is contrasted with de Gourmont for not being able to do what de Gourmont *can*: 'supply the conscious *formulas* of a sensibility *in process of formation*; he [Benda] is rather the ideal scavenger of the rubbish of our time . . . Much of his analysis of the decadence of contemporary French society could be *applied to* London, although differences are *observable* from his *diagnosis*' (*SW* 44).

One must draw attention to Eliot's habitual use of medical-physical metaphors to lend again that curious sense of objectivity to his judgments. In the passages above we have seen *diagnosis*, *pathology* and *faculty*. In addition Eliot constantly sees the activity of thinking as *like* the mechanical operation of an organism: de Gourmont 'scavenges', the spirit of a time is 'flavour', Whibley has 'a healthy appetite' (*SW* 33); Whibley and Wyndham have 'gusto, but gusto is no equivalent for taste; it depends too much on the appetite and digestion of the feeder' (*SW* 40). And 'devour' is a word that occurs more than once.

The following make interesting comparisons:

(h) '. . . precision, a result of concentrated attention to what [one] is writing . . . objectivity and again objectivity, and expression . . .' (*The Letters of Ezra Pound*, ed. D. D. Paige (New York, Harcourt, Brace and Co., 1950), pp. 48–9).

(i) 'Poetry is a sort of inspired mathematics, which gives us equations, not for abstract figures, triangles, spheres and the like, but equations for the human emotions.' (Ezra Pound, *The Spirit of Romance*, p. 5). Quoted in W. K. Wimsatt and Cleanth Brooks, *Literary Criticism: A Short History*, who remark: 'In constructing his ideograph, the poet is as "impersonal" as the scientist.'

(j) 'Eliot's emphasis upon "the generalizing power" and upon the critic's need to objectify, gives the clue to his special kind of classicism.' (Wimsatt and Brooks, p. 659). Again, de Gourmont 'move[d] away from mere impression towards objectivity' (p. 658).

The objectivity here is surely scientific. Impersonality likewise has a scientific affiliation and is connected with dissociation. F. W. Bateson remarks that Eliot got the phrase 'dissociation of sensibility' from de Gourmont, who is speaking of Laforgue: '*dissocier son intelligence de sa sensibilité*' (*Essays in Critical Dissent*, p. 144).

(k) '. . . the classicism of Hulme is a form of objectivism which insists upon clear distinctions between ethical and religious doctrine and poetic composition' (Wimsatt and Brooks, p. 661). Note Hulme's insistence on 'dry hardness', 'simplicity', 'function' and 'structure'.

Are things distinct when the vocabulary of 'the one thing' mingles with that of 'the other'?

NOTE B

Personality and Dissociation

The following supplementary contexts for the word *personality* are juxtaposed in order to reinforce the suggestion that personality itself is often spoken of by Eliot as if it too were something 'out there': objectified. The person watches the personality, with a peculiarly modern self-consciousness—'watching oneself'. ('Je est un autre'—said Rimbaud.) The personality can become something passive that can be manipulated—perhaps into 'role-playing'. There is an inevitable dissociation. All italics are mine.

(a) 'The end of the enjoyment of poetry is a pure contemplation from which all the *accidents* of personal emotion are removed; thus we aim to see the object as it really is . . . And without a labour which is largely a labour of the intelligence, we are unable to attain that stage of vision *amor intellectualis Dei*' (*SW*, 15).

This is like an inversion of Blake's 'seeing not through but *with* the eye'. Blake is active; Eliot passive, as if one would see God by obliterating self. The same motifs recur: the idea of *labour*, the idea of *extinction*.

(b) 'The sentimental person, in whom a work of art arouses all sorts of emotions which have nothing to do with that work of art whatsoever, but are *accidents* of personal association, is an incomplete artist. For in an artist these suggestions . . . which are purely personal, become *fused with* a multitude of other suggestions from multitudinous experience, and *result* in the *production of* a new *object* which is no longer purely personal, because it is a work of art itself' (*SW*, 7).

The tortuous circularity of this can't disguise that fact that no distinction has been made at all. And a mechanical activity (passive) is supposed to be less a matter of 'accident' than association is. However sentimental that may be, it is at least active. The business of *fusing* offers no security that the artist can know what is happening. The catalyst image is not far away.

(c) 'We have to communicate . . . an experience which is not an experience in the ordinary sense, for it may only exist, *formed out of* many personal experiences *ordered in some way* which may be very different from the way of valuation of practical life, in the expression of it' (*The Use of Poetry and the Use of Criticism*, p. 30).

The distinctions between the words 'communicate', 'express' and 'experience' all collapse here. The experience is the expression is the communication. A poem is a poem is a poem.

(d) '. . . in the greatest poetry there is always a hint of something behind, something impersonal, something in relation to which the author has been *no more than the passive* (if not always pure) medium.' (From Eliot's 'Commentary', *The Criterion*, October 1932.)

(e) '. . . a fearful progress of self-consciousness . . .' (UPUC, p. 121. Of Jacques Maritain on Picasso) . . . '[this] progress is not necessarily a progress of higher value . . . (p. 122) . . . the modern mind comprehends every extreme and degree of opinion . . .' (p. 124).

(f) 'One of the reasons for learning at least one foreign language well is that we acquire a kind of supplementary personality; one of the reasons for not acquiring a new language instead of our own is that most of us do not want to become a different person' ('The Social Function of Poetry', *To Criticize the Critic*, p. 19).

A false dilemma. Learning a language needn't result in schizophrenia.

CHAPTER IV

Conclusion: Self and Society

The conditions of self and society which co-operated to make
Eliot a critic of high classical standing, a possessor of the intuition
of genius, were exactly those which at the same time disable him
from the consistency which would raise his criticism even higher
in future estimation. The paradoxical nature of the achievement,
with the multiple paradoxes revolving about the central one, has
been at the centre of the present essay in interpretation. His
impersonality turns out to be rooted in personal exigency; the
representativeness which makes him a figure of permanent import
is peculiarly of a time; the exceptional insights that are the strength
of his criticism are absolutely contingent upon the central weaknesses; the fragmentariness, hesitation, inconsistency and equivo-
cation are part of a whole whose instability is the necessarily
insecure foundation for his clairvoyant sense of his times. This
vision is finally double: for us, a matter of admiration, and regret.
When he sees the consistency of Johnson[1] and admires and praises
it, he can also see—and so indeed do we—that even such an
achievement exacts the price of not being able to see other things.
Eliot, as it were, wishes to see the face and the vase in the perceptual diagram at once. But this is something that eye and mind
cannot see, and that no convention, not even the Metaphysical,
can accommodate. We can only look in one direction at once;
be one thing, and not another. To speak psychologically, that
direction must be *our own*, of our identity, our person. The problem for our understanding of Eliot is partly that of how a healthy
wholeness can feel for and understand the fragmented temperament. To be *in* one condition prohibits the others.[2] Or, to bring
the matter quickly back to the position of the modern poet, and
thereby to Eliot:

> The modern poet has committed himself to the task of under-
> standing experience in its immediacy. He has neglected the

armature of the priest—the precautionary wisdom of tradition —and often, the inculcated respect for literary models. But therefore, he only, and more strongly, knows the need of mediation.[3]

There, too, in Hartman's expression of it, is the vision and the penalty at once: the paradox. The object of his reflections is Rilke, but they help us to see the predicament of Eliot more clearly. *He* cannot be said to have neglected any of the matters (he is in our time the exemplar, in English, of attention to them) but at the same time he must have feared that to enter fully into the parts of royalist, classicist, conservative, would entail some later-Wordsworthian hardening of the sensibilities. Gain of security might mean the loss of intuitive understanding—or would it? How do you know until you have tried—and yet, if you should try —and the fear is proved? Only loss could confirm the possibility. The example of Rilke (who is mentioned only in passing by Eliot —strangely enough), or Valéry does present itself in his way:

> the will to experience all things without choice or refusal and in their immediacy is not fully realized even by Rilke ... the poet is compelled to find ... symbols, and one of them is a mirror, the impersonal mirror ... For it enables the observer oppressed by experiences he cannot shake off ... both to represent these fully and to deny them any personal significance. He will look in this mirror ... and he will say—not 'this refers to me' but—*this is* ('*nicht: das bin ich; nein: dies ist*').[4]

Rilke took on the burden of 'experiencing all things' with a more naked determination than Eliot—a singleness of purpose which is reflected in his resistance to any form of religion-as-institution, or politics-as-institution, and also in his expressed love of the *example* of Christ along with his rejection of the doctrine of Christ as mediator between man and God. To be a poet, to re-confirm praise of the Creator, the poet himself is to become the mediator, through language, of what he tries to experience without the protective resistance of any 'armature' at all. Nothing must interpose between the self and 'reality'; in the conjunction of the two one can at last say 'dies ist'. *One* is *at one*. The mode for the utterance of such knowledge is to be the intensified im-

personal descriptive: some passages of Wordsworth conform to
the purpose. But at the same time the legend of Perseus and Medusa
suggests what may happen to those who try to dispense with the
mediating conventions that are a necessary part of our human
world. The way in which Eliot recurs again and again in his
criticism (both literary and social) to just this question of conventions—the essay on Massinger is particularly important in this
respect—suggests an awareness of the danger that was perhaps
associated with a deeper fear. He did not dare, as it were, to eat
Cézanne's apple of knowledge, or to release himself to the example
of Lawrence. His uneasiness with the latter, notoriously expressed
in *After Strange Gods*,[5] does however convey a sense of attraction-
with-repulsion. On the one hand he could not separate *direct*
expression from 'self-expression' in his own pejorative sense; and
yet, as a coeval and descendant of Rilke, Valéry and Lawrence,
there are many marks in his own poetry of a similar effort at
directness. The 'technique' of *The Waste Land* is a way of trying
to express—as in the opening sections of Rilke's *Notebooks of
Malte Laurids Brigge*—the direct burden on a naked sensibility of
the experience of the modern city and of an essentially convention-
less 'society' where there was still *some* 'precautionary wisdom' to
be found in literary tradition. There is, too, the 'technique for
sincerity' of the *Four Quartets*. And again, there are parallels to be
drawn between Rilke's gradual lifting of himself towards the
celebration of life ('preisen') in the *Duino Elegies* and the *Sonnets
to Orpheus* and Eliot's

> I rejoice, having to construct
> > something/
> Upon which to rejoice[6]

and his

> I made this, I have forgotten
> And remember . . .
> Made this unknowing, half-conscious, unknown,
> > my own.[7]

Here, for our purpose, the emphasis should fall on the last two
words: in the past century thoughtful and sensitive human beings
have had to *find*, for themselves, something to praise. It has not
been 'given'.

From 'Tradition and the Individual Talent', at the same time, we can interpret Impersonality as a suspension of conscious intellect in order to admit something like Rilke's direct intuition, which takes its terms from modern science (a science which has absolutes of its own, for example 'to explain the secret of life')[8] rather than religion. However, it is hard to imagine that any 'absolute' of 'unmediated vision' could be fundamentally at one with the final purposes of modern scientific method. Eliot, in another of his guises, might well have remarked that both of these ends were manifestations of a quite peculiar modern *hubris*.

With the hindsight of subsequent history no-one would find it easy to say that Eliot's instinctive need for the conventional was wrong—that his 'addiction'[9] to Dante (the armature of a coherence between poetry, philosophy and dogma) was quite misguided. Perhaps if he had brought himself to say that Chaucer belonged to a saner world than Lawrence; that the latter, as Eliot himself, still carried marks of the pathologies of his time—then he would have said something more helpful to a still Faustian posterity. He would then, too, have been fairer to the Lawrence who wrote the parable of what happens to human personality when it removed itself from the human world into the isolated apprehension of nature: *The Man Who Loved Islands*. But Eliot did not, or could not, say these things. He was *of* that time, and it would anyway have required a more stable insight into himself than he possessed.

Though he knew, and often said, that the human world needs conventions, and though he knew that there are things beyond these conventions that cannot be known, he did not ever seem to be able to see the full significance of the knowledge. That would have meant seeing its significance for himself, and might have meant a further self-exposure. But it might, too, have meant a greater stability. His tendency to write of authors who were immediately interesting to him is one expression of an inner *need*[10] the general significance of which isn't quite grasped for himself. While it gives us the finest perceptions it at the same time involves the persistent disconnectedness that has been noted in my two central chapters:

In reviewing my own early criticism, I am struck by the degree to which it was conditioned by the state of literature at the time at which it was written, as well as by the stage of maturity at which I had been exposed, and by the occasion of each essay.[11]

From the standpoint of this later and rather condescending *persona*, Eliot makes it sound like a set of accidents. To be so conditioned would be to be contained-within. Although Eliot took his opportunities marvellously well there is still an element of opportunism about the performance—a sudden high-wire walk. Throughout the essays, in retrospect, Eliot, younger or older, never quite lifts himself sufficiently *above* his subjects to achieve the kind of conspectus which would have implied a stabilized relation between a number of matters that were in fact never settled. Among these, for example, there is the irregularity of his attentions to Shakespeare, the apparent preference for Dante over the former, the absence of reference to English medieval literature. And all of this entails consequences for his general view of society. Without the settlement being made, the reader feels an absence: of essential groundings within the criticism of connections between the fine things that *are* present.[12] It is another aspect of fragmentariness; an echo of the failed relation between *personality* and *impersonality*. Unable, unlike Lawrence, to build out of his own personality an inclusive judgment of his age which would distance the age and reduce its disabling effects, he remained subject to it and them.

The best brief statement of those effects and of their consequences for the personality is given by van Heerikhuizen in his book on Rilke:

The nineteenth century, shortly characterized, can be seen as a time of shattered structures, of centrifugal forces, of sharp contrasts in immediate juxtaposition. The various parts of mental and spiritual life that had, until the nineteenth century, been united in one, even if weakening tradition, now began to diverge, to become independent of one another ... [The] expansion [of scientific habits of thought] was peculiarly glorious in that possibilities seemed infinite ... and peculiarly formidable because bridges had to be burnt, the human personality in its ancient harmonious conception to be discarded ...

The *loss of the conception of personality* as the centre of the universal forces from which the universe itself was governed presents the psychological aspect of the loss of the traditional world picture ... Because of this loss, the new pictures were coloured with an extreme pessimism ... *and often these views were held simultaneously, for extremes are mysteriously linked* and tend to swing from one to the other with no diminution of their contrasts.

From the middle of the century, the materialistic-positivistic trend, which derived mind from matter and hence led in the direction of a levelling under-estimation of the mind, increasingly prevailed. Followed to its logical conclusion this total denial of human self-determination led to *a weakening of volitional life* and into pessimism ... *Specialization supervened as a means of self-preservation.*[13] (My italics.)

Out of the microcosm of 'Tradition and the Individual Talent' one can read back into the poetry with which one would otherwise begin, and by implication into the life, an Eliot at once fighting against and reflecting the tendencies of his time: tendencies which (as with any period, better or worse) are *within* each single one of us that the times contain; individuals who *can* where necessary release themselves from its grip.[14] The analysis of Eliot's attitude towards personality-impersonality have perhaps shown something of all this: the 'weakening of the volitional life' going with unsettled and consequently equivocal attitudes; those in turn leading to the assumption of masking roles, or momentary ventriloquisms, when under pressure: these being forms of the 'specialization' which supervenes as self-preservation. Then, the 'loss of a conception of personality' goes with a failure of confidence or nerve even at moments of essential self-assertion against the materialist-positivist trends of his time. This in turn is a part of Eliot's ability to hold 'essentially contradictory' views without resolving them; allowing them to swing from one side to the other where 'extremes are mysteriously linked' in what we have consistently noted as the paradoxical nature of the constatation. Such a *gestalt* is not open to 'a merely intellectual interest':[15] the originating life, the personality, *must* be entered.

SELF-PROTECTION AND 'THE POSSIBILITY OF RELEASE'

A deeper sense of Eliot's vulnerability (the personal sources of which, focussing interpretation upon the criticism only, I have avoided direct reference to) should entail a keener appreciation of the will to life which opposed itself within him to the debilitating influences at the very same time as his vulnerability *to* them made him an extraordinarily representative reflector *of* them. In the face of the testimony that comes from the criticism and the poetry, the word 'heroic' won't seem out of place. It is, interestingly enough, used both by F. R. Leavis, in 'Eliot's Classical Standing' and elsewhere:

> I see Eliot's creative career as a sustained, heroic and indefatigably resourceful quest of a profound sincerity of the most difficult kind. The heroism is that of genius.[16]

and also by Heerikhuizen, of Rilke:

> The life of Rilke must be entered: its fundamental problems springing from his times, its heroic human struggle and its possibility of release rooted deeply in his own being.[17]

And such a deepened appreciation will inevitably lead us to some sympathetic qualifications, even as we relish their force, of remarks (again supplementing Eliot's own on the subject of knowledge) such as those of Wyndham Lewis':

> The 'burden of information and consciousness' does in fact over-balance the man of today, in many instances. What with the consciousness or the 'sense' of the past, and the labour of gathering 'information' about it, to enable it to become an integral part of the present, those who succumbed to the theory of Mr Pound or Mr Eliot should scarcely expect not to lose coherence—they must expect to sacrifice more and more of that 'self' or 'personality' which is merely living adequately at any given moment, to become an 'impersonal' rendezvous for two-dimensional phantoms, and to look more or less like a bric-a-brac shop, observed from the outside.[18]

It is hard not to agree—with its premonition of Marcuse. So much of the theorizing of the time—Pound, Hulme, Eliot, Valéry, de

Gourmont—does look like that, now: except that the contents of
the shop have come more to seem like totems collected by an
eccentric necessity. Kathleen Nott, in her much less telling way,
does not see *enough* of what is there to be seen:

> when we decipher, as we often do, another piece of Mr Eliot's
> deliberate mosaic of quotation, we experience some, no doubt
> irrational, disappointment, because after all we were uncon-
> sciously looking for Eliot . . .[19]

and again: 'Mr Eliot manifests himself with baffling discontinuity . . .'[20] Throughout her essay irritation obscures Miss Nott's
proper understanding, and with it, the *proper* irritation. Of course,
we don't want an improper or sentimental sympathy for Eliot,
either; there has been enough of that, and it needs the corrective.
But Miss Nott and Wyndham Lewis have a 'line' which does not
really incorporate an understanding of their *own* position, a sight
of the world which included Eliot as including them also—and a
recognition that the inclusion imposes similar disabilities: here of
reaction (the 'swing from one to the other'). In reaction of this
kind, the critic is not free enough. One way of saying so is to
remark that the kind of impersonality that might release us from
'personality' in Eliot's sense is quite different from that expressed
in 'Tradition'. The reflex-reaction there is one of *conformity*—to
tones, to roles, to the *sound* of science. And this even though
science analyses, fragments; cannot give coherence, or wholeness
or vision of itself.[21] These things exist in it when it is subservient
to them—as in ancient Greece. When the idea of personality is
referred to it, it is the cause of division: what follows psycho-
analysis? Eliot, throughout his life in criticism and poetry was
trying to create the wholeness of poems at a time when the relationship was reversed, when poetic-intuitive life was subordinated
to the measure of science (and science in a state of optimism) and
its 'objective' reducing and separating method. His work in fact
is continuous with Donne's exclamation in *The First Anniversary*
that when 'She' is dead, 'what fragmentary rubbish this world is'.
But by Eliot's time dissociation is trying to cure dissociation, and
does not know that that is what it is trying to do. We are a long
way before Polanyi, Popper, Kuhn, Grene or Roszak. Finally,
wholeness was not within his more-than-temporary grasp. Hugh

Kenner's quick completion of Eliot's remark on Henry Adams, tells us a great deal: ' "Wherever this man stepped, the ground did not simply give way, it flew into particles"; he might have been an impressionable student of Bradley.'[22] It is one of Eliot's tellingly expressive metaphors (the vehicle is scientific) whose force refers us as much, or more, to Eliot as to his subject. He, *seeing-in* to his subjects, is their real tenor. It is the same when he remarks of Joyce that one has the sense 'of eveything happening at once'[23] with being 'too conscious, and conscious of too much'. This is a world, apparently, from which a sure source of personality has seemed to drop out through the interstices between the fragments, along with any vision that sustains and gives coherence. Such a supposition is supported by Wollheim's remarks (p. 87) about the curiously empty idea of mind to which Eliot may have been influenced through Bradley, who is interpreted by Eliot as saying:

> The real flower, we can say, will be the sum of effects—its actual effects upon other entities—and this sum must form a system, must somehow hang together.[24]

Put that way the phrases have an eerily quantitative effect, with its *somehow*, its *system*, its *totality* (rather than *whole*) and with the echo of the saying about a thing being the sum of its parts—with the *more than* missing. Things are named or numbered, but have no expressed relation, though that is what is most wanted. It is as if one could name all the personality-'factors' (as used to be done in I.Q. testing) and say that the personality is the sum of them, or describe all the elements of a sentence linguistically and say that *that* is what the sentence *means*. The quantitative naming of effects and of parts takes away the sense of relation—and the sense of Personality (a unique set of relations) suffers. Confidence goes, the sense of continuity and stability cannot subsist, the notion of wholeness crumbles: 'I can connect/Nothing with nothing'.[25]

Gertrude Patterson's comment is understandable:

> Eliot's whole theory of the impersonality of art, and moreover his refusal to recognize the personality of the poet, the sole qualification for artistic practice, are difficult to reconcile with the superb confidence of the Romantic poet.[26]

Without a certain continuing confidence in its self, any human being is in a sorry condition. From Romanticism onward, a lack of life-confidence has been a characteristic of literature (Tennyson, Clough, Arnold), and in Eliot's time the condition appears to have become radical. In this respect he looks forward to what was to come rather than, like Lawrence, being a part of what was going, while knowing that it *was* going. It is interesting, remembering Eliot's origins, to reflect on this:

> ... for our grandparents a 'House', a 'Well', a familiar tower, their very dress, their cloak, was infinitely more, infinitely more intimate; almost everywhere a vessel in which they found and stored humanity. Now there come crowding over from America empty, indifferent things, pseudo-things, dummy life ... The animated, experienced things that share our lives are coming to an end and cannot be replaced.[27]

With his only-provisional confidence, the need for support was strong—in tradition, in classicism, in dogma. And in addition—it is just one more paradox as the coin turns over and its axis changes angle—the exigency which intensified the insight made him equally susceptible to influences actually unhelpful. One can see the influence of Bradley in this way; 'one of the most important deposits of Bradleyism in Eliot is visible in the disarmingly hesitant and fragmentary way in which he makes a point, or expresses a conviction.'[28] But which would have come first—the disposition or the example? What reinforced what? In view of Eliot's declaration about what he retained from Bradley—'a style', and in view too of Kenner's further comment that 'it is precisely as a stain, imparting colour to all else that passes through, that Bradley is most discernible in Eliot's poetic sensibility',[29] we can trust our sense to be justified that he was not so much interested in 'ideas', the intellectual interest, as in confirmations of his own intuition.

These inclinations of Eliot's have, presumably, a subterranean connection with his general susceptibility to impression (that of a poet) which made him so clairvoyantly adept in quotation, or at adapting quotation to his own ends. It is an extraordinary and rather eerie spectacle, the way in which the semi-conscious roots of sensibility reach down for what is needed, as the plant struggles up for light: both vulnerable and determined. One can see the trait here:

> Il y a une beauté littéraire, impersonelle en quelque sorte, par-faitement distincte de l'auteur lui-meme et de son organisation, beauté, qui a sa raison d'être et ses lois, dont la critique est tenue de rendre compte. Et si la critique considère cette tache comme au-dessous d'elle, si c'est affaire a la rhétorique et a ce que Sainte-Beuve appelle dédaigneusement les Quintilien, alors la rhétorique a du bon et les Quintilien ne sont pas à dédaigner.

This, by Othenin d'Haussonville, is quoted in 'Imperfect Critics' (*The Sacred Wood*, p. 42). One might think it a translation into French of something by Eliot himself. Given the sensibility, who knows how much Eliot might owe to this snatch of style—or another? He might flinch from, or move towards, anything. Despite all his intention towards impersonality—and with the classicism it really indicates a will to invulnerability—one can see at the same time a poetic sensibility working with peculiar naked-ness and obviousness. The two things, of course, go together: and one must see both. At the same time, he would want to protect himself against our insight.

Bradley was one of those who *expressed* something for him, through whom Eliot could express himself without it being *him-self*: he comes close to it and takes its 'colouring'. In this, however, insecurity is not so likely to be guarded-against as confirmed, fragmentariness and dissociation at most recognized. In Eliot, as in our own period, there is still taking place 'the disintegrating collision in a sensitive mind of the old tradition and the new learning',[30] except that, by 1900, the cultural conditions did not even present the comfort of clear dualities, however much they might be created by oppositions of classicism to Romanticism (see above, Chapter II, n. 38).

Eliot's interests in fact are the reverse of theoretic; he knew that his life was bound up with the life of his culture, with the life of his literature: he knew that everybody's life was bound up in that way. He was afraid of death, which is best understood as living death:

> The trouble of the modern age is not merely the inability to believe certain things about God and man which our fore-

fathers believed, but the inability to *feel* towards God and man
as they did ... what I am apprehensive of is death. It is ...
possible that the feeling for poetry, and the feelings that are the
material of poetry, may disappear everywhere: which might
perhaps help to facilitate that unification of the world which
some people consider desirable for its own sake.[31]

The weary disdain audible in the last part of the last sentence is
not pleasant; nor is it, again, a good sign that Eliot speaks of
feelings as 'materials', or that he is able to speak of poetry in the
title of the essay as having a 'social function', as though the phrase
did not fit all too easily with the idea of social engineering ...
but still, Eliot is speaking directly to everyone, here. The poet is
not separate from the man, his life is ours, he is for the moment a
man speaking to men. It is the fears that give conviction to the
criticism—as they might give a strong conviction to academic
teaching or to journalism-reviewing. In the present state of English
literature we might well ask ourselves how near we are to the
condition that Eliot foresaw.[32] What is, after all, the connection
between having a literature and having an identity—national or
personal? Can you have one, as fully as one would wish, without
the other?:

> The greatest single cultural problem we face, assuming that we
> physically survive: that is, how to use a heritage ... how to
> grow by means of it, how to acquire our own 'identities', how
> to be ourselves.[33]

And Bate goes on to speak of the conflict of the modern, of the
split in our sense of what to do with ourselves: 'In the arts the
split is widening. The essence of neurosis is conflict.'

Eliot speaks out of that neurosis and conflict: and he could not
have spoken so remarkably if they had not been more than just
his own. His poetic susceptibility is impersonal and personal,
though the two rarely unite in the consistent, Wordsworthian
confidence; 'binding together by passion and knowledge'. But
Wordsworth could not have foreseen this likelihood:

> if I were told that no more poetry was being written in (say)
> the Norwegian language ... I should regard it as a spot of
> malady which was likely to spread over the whole continent;

the beginning of a decline which would mean that people everywhere would cease to be able to express, and consequently be able to feel, the emotions of civilized beings.[34]

For the critic of the critic, for us, one problem is how much responsibility to lay upon Eliot and *how* to lay it on him? How much is personal weakness—still bearing in mind that there is a paradoxical connection between the weaknesses and the sharpest insights. Of course, the stresses and tensions referred to by Bate focus in the person. And yet, despite a strong sense of agreement and relief that it is at least being said awakened by Yvor Winters' comment that

> Eliot, in brief, has surrendered to the *acedia* which Baudelaire was able to judge; Eliot suffers from the delusion that he is judging it when he is merely exhibiting it . . . being unaware of his own contradictions, he is able to make a virtue of what appears to be private spiritual laziness; he is able to enjoy at one and the same time the pleasure of indulgence and the dignity of disapproval.[35]

—despite our sense that Eliot very often deserves these (more precisely 'Johnsonian') strictures, that Winters' resistance is the kind we all need—yet there is something present in the judgment that in its turn needs to be resisted. As with Kathleen Nott's comments, there is too much reaction in it, as there is too in some of the criticism made by F. R. Leavis in his intricate and delicate exposition of the 'case' of Eliot in *The Living Principle*.[36] Eliot's 'case' is not just his. One wants to resist a confidence that is not quite of the right kind, wanting in sufficient sympathy of expression. The criticism made of Professor Chalker's sense of Eliot's own Johnsonianism must still hold: the more the style is like that of Johnson, the less it is of our own time. There is a distance, really, of more than a century, between Winters and Eliot. Given this—and of course there is a danger for us in going too near—it is difficult to take full significance of Eliot for ourselves, and thus to see our own positions. To see them better makes it possible for us to free ourselves and our criticism rather more from the self-protectiveness that can on occasion disguise itself in the defence of principle,[37] or can cover itself with the carapace of a theory or of a professional

manner. Eliot's predicament is our predicament; the aetiology of
his sensibility is the most discomfitingly faithful register that we
have of the times, despite his own attempts at disguise. It is one
reason why he is still a central figure; precisely because he was
not, like the Metaphysicals he admired,

> utterly committed to the world of spiritual meaning and value:
> [where] the other lesser worlds, 'divided' but not isolated, were
> all mutually related and harmonised in a hierarchy of value
> which was accepted as no mere imposition of the interpreting
> mind but an accurate pattern of ultimate spiritual reality.[38]

Because he *was* the inhabitant of worlds that had divided, when,

> physical science, discarding theological interpretation, sets up
> on its own account, when the other secular activities follow
> suit and religion itself becomes an isolated sphere. Then the
> mind can no longer range among them, achieving fruitful
> relationships, since there is no coordinating ultimate *principle*
> upon which relationships can be grounded—only a common
> *method*, *assimilating* the various fields of study without *relating*
> them either in correspondence or organically. And the method
> itself, originating in the special requirements of one subordinate
> sphere, that of the lowest, inanimate, order of being, was
> extended to the higher spheres quite unwarrantably.[39]

SEEING ELIOT: SEEING OURSELVES

It is for the above reasons that it has been necessary to insist that a
scholarly attentiveness is not enough in the reading of Eliot's
essays, and to point to some theoretical criticism, some 'approaches'
as examples of just that. They too act as dissociations; specialisms
as method, protection, distance. They don't permit enough truth;
there are truths beyond them that they can't cope with—as there
are beyond science itself. When that is seen clearly then we have
a firmer notion of what our methods *can* tell us. To put oneself
'inside' a method is to separate oneself, to specialize our wholeness
for an end, and consequently to separate ourselves from the
wholeness or the complexity we bring ourselves to. Keeping ourselves *within* we limit the self, give it a form which is not of the

whole self (as in effect Eliot did in the second part of 'Tradition and the Individual Talent').[40] From within, of course, we can find particular and useful explications to make: with Eliot it is not too difficult to discover something to say of that sort. His own taste for the odd and recondite can encourage the unraveller in all of us. But the real force of the criticism *is* expressive; poetic and personal; and this must refer back with all its contradiction, to the man, and then beyond. There is a truth to the criticism that Eliot was unaware of. He was unaware of his incoherence, no doubt; and many critics have pointed it out: but still there is a coherence beneath that surface. We move from measurement by straight-edge to, nowadays, a necessarily more tortuous interpretation.

A criticism that isn't reaction will try to express the fullest truth about the case; it will work towards the ends towards which Eliot was working and which are always hard to achieve: a wholeness of judgment which is at the same time a wholeness or balance of personality. Such a criticism will see its own position. It will try not simply to reflect its times and leave succeeding times to look back and note that fact: it will try to get above them, as Eliot on occasion did, at the same time as it knows it is *of* them. If its subject is Eliot it will see him as both a prisoner and as someone with a clairvoyant understanding of the nature of his own prison—as a particular kind of intelligence rare in any society:

> If a captive mind is unaware of being in prison, it is living in error. If it has recognized the fact, even for the tenth of a second, and then quickly forgotten it in order to avoid the suffering, it is living in falsehood. Men of the most brilliant intelligence can be born, live, and die in error and falsehood. In them, intelligence is neither a good, nor even an asset. The difference between more or less intelligent men is like the difference between criminals condemned to life imprisonment in smaller or larger cells. The intelligent man who is proud of his intelligence is like a condemned man who is proud of his large cell.[41]

A true attempt at such criticism will always take such statements of ends as at once challenges and as accusations of failure. Feeling that, it will want to praise Eliot for whatever it was in him that wished to be out of his prison, and it will try to see the nature of the prison—the social world inhabited by the poet. In Eliot's case, it will want to sympathize. It will see the 'deceptive chaos',[42] but faced with its own general standard of truth, it won't wish to exculpate Eliot's failures by social 'explanations': the responsibility still exists. Criticism should have the peculiar combination of clarity and sympathy which will be the result of a certain conviction or vision. It will have an idea of the kind of sense and order that a notion of the good, or of truth, gives; then, having that sense, will wish to take such remarks as Santayana's: 'Our poets are things of shreds and patches: they give us episodes and studies ... they have no total vision ...'[43] and will want to ask of our poetry and criticism whether this is so, why, in what way has the poet met his world—in resistance or submission—what is the nature of these shreds and patches? And, in dealing with a poet as close to ourselves as Eliot, such a criticism will not wish to evade the possibility that our poetry and criticism itself will be affected by similar conditions; that we may be suffering, most of us, from comparable disabilities, whose paradoxical nature is to prevent us from seeing *ourselves* in Eliot, and our conformity to the conditions which he tried to resist, as retrospective complicity.

*   ★   *

These pages have attempted to propose and perform a general critical activity which, believing in the importance of serious thought in ordinary language about the relation between self-poet and society-world, might begin to meet the kind of objection to Eliot's work that expresses itself in repugnance and dismissal, and to reinstate Eliot in the sympathy of a public that seems to be increasingly deciding that it need not pay as much attention to him as has been paid in the past. It is only by such an attempt that his criticism—or ours—can be claimed as a living issue, rather than a theoretical one. One consequence of this activity is that the critic will have to concentrate on the living tissue in the work, and not try to make the whole live by *making sense of* it: and the only way of deciding which *is* the living tissue is by reading the criticism as literature: through response and the testing of response. 'Method' can't do it. An attentive reading of the essays reveals, I believe, something split in the middle ('Tradition' is the clearest sign of the fault) that Eliot never seems to have clearly recognized and that consequently he went on perpetuating.[44] Once we have recognized it and tried to explain it, we find it running into a tracery of instability throughout the criticism. The active personality is continually being betrayed by the passive, thought and feeling separate—and then are united in 'reconciliations'. As we have noted, Eliot rarely expressed the idea of wholeness. Even when he does:

> When the poet's mind is perfectly equipped for its task, it is constantly amalgamating disparate experience; the ordinary man's experience is chaotic, irregular, fragmentary. The latter falls in love, or reads Spinoza, and these two experiences have nothing to do with each other, or with the noise of the typewriter or the smell of cooking; in the mind of the poet these experiences are always forming new wholes.[45]

—even here, where the notion of wholeness is expressed in a way that might have served Eliot as a paradigm for wholeness of personality, his expression entails division upon division. In the last three lines Eliot enacts for us what may happen in the creating mind: we see it happening, and it is invigorating; we know better what it means, and what we *want*. And the wanting is active. But the passage is infected with its own denial: the world is full of disparate experience (as though the *experiencer* is not enough of an entity to give it any shape); the mind is 'equipped', things are 'amalgamated'; the poet is separated from the 'ordinary man', and this ordinary man is such an extraordinary ordinary man (he reads Spinoza) that it leaves very few of the elect who are free from the disability of being only capable of fragmentary experience. And what does Eliot think that his readers will think of the way he speaks of them? Is he unaware of the possibility of insult? Is that not itself a dissociation? If we *react*—it is surely understandable. We are left with a vivid image of an experience (it tells us how we *do*, ordinary men, remember things)—but it is in a negative form. Not I *can* do: but the rest of you *can't*. The positive, so oddly and as so often, contained within the negative. It *is* characteristic:

> No sensible author, in the midst of something that he is trying to write, can stop to consider whether he is going to be romantic

or the opposite. At the moment when one writes one is what one is,

(at which point one feels the hope of an agreement rising; but the recoil is on:)

and the damage of a lifetime, and of having been born into an unsettled society, cannot be repaired at the moment of composition.[46]

This is moving again. We know that Eliot is talking about himself, by implication. But is composition 'just a moment'? Do we not write *to* repair ourselves? Is not this a curiously *romantic* idea, near to 'self-expression'? Would not a properly general argument, or theory, add the compensating case where there is not so much damage to be repaired? Once again, in fact, the general is muddled by the personal—the variety of the personal which at other times Eliot spoke against. He cannot, on the one hand say: 'this is my own case', but tries to impersonalize the matter through a large generalization. It is another form of escape from self. Eliot tries to hide, when finally, one cannot hide. And on Eliot's own presentation of 'the poet' we cannot take this either as the 'criticism of a poet', 'the offshoot of his poetry workshop'. It is the 'man who suffers' who is speaking, but too nakedly for criticism. We hear an insecurity: *personal* and *impersonal* out of relation.

Security would not have needed the defensive hauteur that Eliot adopted on so many occasions. Corresponding to the escape are the barriers of manner, role-playing, class-colouring, orthodoxy, even 'theory'. To understand this is to begin to return Eliot to the condition of a man speaking to men, but one who reveals himself in his effort to hide, the inevitable and recurrent paradox. We may think that his poetry and criticism are often

... torn between his desire to reveal himself and his desire to conceal himself. We all share this problem with him, and we have all arrived at a more or less satisfactory solution. We have our secrets and our needs to confess. We may remember how, in childhood, adults were at first able to look right through us, and into us, and what an accomplishment it was when we, in fear and trembling, could tell our first lie, and make, for ourselves, the discovery that we are irredeemably alone in certain respects, and we know that within the territory of ourselves there can only be our footprints.[47]

Eliot never quite arrived at a 'satisfactory solution'—which was often a source of strength for the poetry and criticism, through the consequent intensity of feeling. Following the footprints through Eliot's criticism in this way we can see that it is of a piece with the poetry, that it needs to be read in essentially the same way. The two are continuous, both are continuous with the man, the man is continuous with his time. His 'theory' has none of the 'objective' status that the term suggests (Wordsworth's use of the word 'theory' in his essay of 1800, the Preface to *Lyrical Ballads* is quite different):[48] it is an attempt to resist the fragmentation of personality that Eliot saw in the world: '*Le monde moderne avilit. It also provincializes, and it can also corrupt.*'[49] It is possible to read 'provincializes' as meaning that when there is no cultural centre we are all provincial, separated. But then, that need not be a bad thing: the case of Lawrence has to be faced again. But Eliot looks forward, and it may be that a great deal of the literature of our own time—though it is hard to bear the admission—may in the longer run seem fragmentary: inner and outer worlds echoing one another again.[50]

If the 'theory' of impersonality can be read in this way, so too can the equally-celebrated 'theory' of the dissociation of sensibility in the essay on 'The Metaphysical Poets'. Here Eliot can say something about himself without saying it personally—even though it is 'something from which we have never recovered'. There were things which Eliot knew long before others, with a peculiar intensity which seems to have been a condition of other areas of unawareness: the need for escape into unconsciousness conspiring to hold back the reasoning mind from fulfilling its task. The circle of understanding—inner with outer—is not joined. In this way, but only in this way, one can see the essays as 'poet's criticism'; but to have to do so much work for oneself and others and then to see the final connections unmade is to see at once the burden, the failure and the reasons; to join criticism with a proper sympathy.

*   *   *

Self-sacrifice, surrender; detachment-from, attachment-to; orthodoxies, conventions, habits, manners, forms, modes: in the constant exchange between their presence and the presence of a Self,
between *the* Other, otherness, difference and the single individual;
both come into being through the common language. Neither
can exist properly without the other—and there are periods in
history when the collapse of forms removes the necessary opposition to the self. Eliot had an acute sense of this.

The direction his thought might have taken if he had had the
particular kind of strength—but he might not then have been the
poet he was—can be found here:

> So far from its being his person, what is sacred in a human
> being is the impersonal in him.
>
> Everything which is impersonal in man is sacred, and nothing
> else.
>
> In our days, when writers and scientists have so oddly usurped
> the place of priests, the public acknowledges, with a totally
> unjustified docility, that the artistic and scientific faculties are
> sacred . . . If any reason is felt to be called for, people allege that
> the free play of these faculties is one of the highest manifesta-
> tions of the human personality.
>
> Often it is indeed, no more than that. In which case it is easy
> to see how much it is worth and what can be expected from it
> . . .
>
> What is sacred in science is truth; what is sacred in art is
> beauty. Truth and beauty are impersonal. All this is too
> obvious.[51]

So close to Eliot, and so far away. This wasn't obvious to Eliot,
who tried to use an idea of impersonality detached from a notion
of the sacred; and who even, at one point in his career, tried to
express it in the terminology of a science from which the subject,
the person, let alone the sacred, has been expelled in the interests
of 'objectivity'. It was no accident that Eliot wrote out of a culture
for which science, in a state of confidence, provided the chief
reference for the word 'truth', before it became clearer that
science too changes its nature as our ultimate *'what for'* changes;
that there are ideas of truth to which science refers itself.

The general conditions, involving a depreciation of poetry and the intuitive life, may have helped Eliot to mislead himself into thinking (dualistically again) that *impersonality* is the opposite of *personality*, when it need not be. Instead it can be a transformation of personality where personality does *not* extinguish itself; an expansion, free from the ego-selfhood, when both terms, essential for ordinary discourse (without *both* we would not know what we were talking about) become superfluous. Then we think, instinctively, not of a Middleton, or of a Dunbar, or of the ballads with which Dunbar has so much in common, or of the impersonalities of social, or socialist, realism, or of naturalism: but of Shakespeare, or Chaucer, or Herbert, or Tolstoy, all personal *and* impersonal but in differing relations, for all of whom neither word is enough. True personality and true impersonality are the same thing.

BIBLIOGRAPHY

I

The editions of Eliot's critical essays referred to throughout this essay have been as follows:

The Sacred Wood. London: Methuen, first published 1920; University Paperback edition of 1928 reprint, with preface.
Selected Essays. London: Faber and Faber, first published 1932; edition of 1951.
The Use of Poetry and the Use of Criticism. London: Faber and Faber, first published 1933; paperback reprint of 1968.
After Strange Gods. London: Faber and Faber, 1934.
Notes towards the Definition of Culture. London: Faber and Faber, first published 1948, reprint of 1962.
On Poetry and Poets. London: Faber and Faber, 1957.
Knowledge and Experience in the Philosophy of F. H. Bradley. London: Faber and Faber, 1964.
To Criticize the Critic. London: Faber and Faber, 1965.

II

The standard bibliography of Eliot's writing is:

Gallup, Donald. *T. S. Eliot: a Bibliography*. London: Faber and Faber, 1969.
Also useful, for writings on Eliot, is:
Martin, Mildred. *A Half-Century of Eliot Criticism. An Annotated Bibliography of Books and Articles in English, 1916–1965*. Lewisburg: Bucknell University Press, 1972.

III

The several references to the history and philosophy of science have their source in conversations with colleagues teaching on courses where such reference has to be made, and from some consequent familiarity with the changes in ideas in the philosophy of science. Relevant books here are:

Butterfield, Sir H. *The Origins of Modern Science, 1300–1800*. London: Bell, 1949.
Grene, Marjorie. *The Knower and the Known*. London: Faber and Faber, 1966.

Koestler, Arthur. *The Ghost in the Machine.* London: Hutchinson, 1967.

—. *The Sleepwalkers.* London: Hutchinson, 1968.

—. *The Act of Creation.* London: Hutchinson, 1969.

Kuhn, Thomas. *The Structure of Scientific Revolutions.* Chicago: Chicago University Press, 1970.

Polanyi, Michael. *Personal Knowledge: Towards a post-critical philosophy.* London: Routledge and Kegan Paul, 1958.

Popper, Sir Karl. *The Logic of Scientific Discovery.* London: Hutchinson, 1968.

Roszak, Theodore. *Where the Wasteland Ends.* London: Faber and Faber, 1973.

IV

Other References

I have listed below those sources from which I have drawn something, either in agreement or disagreement, even though I have not quoted directly from some of them.

Allan, Mowbray. *T. S. Eliot's Impersonal Theory of Poetry.* Lewisburg: Bucknell University Press, 1972.

Austin, Allen. *T. S. Eliot, the Literary and Social Criticism.* Bloomington: Indiana University Press, 1971.

Barfield, Owen. *Saving the Appearances: a Study in Idolatry.* New York: Harcourt, Brace and World, n.d.

Bate, Walter Jackson. *The Burden of the Past and the English Poet.* London: Chatto and Windus, 1971.

Bateson, F. W. *Essays in Critical Dissent.* London: Longman, 1972.

—. Obituary note on James Smith. *Essays in Criticism,* xxii (1972), pp. 447–8.

Bergonzi, Bernard. *T. S. Eliot.* New York: Macmillan, 1972.

Bethell, S. L. *The Cultural Revolution of the XVII Century.* London, Dennis Dobson, 1953.

Black, Michael. 'That Which Is Perfectly Ourselves', *The Human World,* 6 (Feb. 1972), pp. 3–16.

Bradbury, Malcolm and Palmer, David. *Contemporary Criticism.* London: Edward Arnold, 1970.

Braybrooke, N. (ed.) *T. S. Eliot, a symposium for his 70th birthday.* London: Rupert Hart-Davis, 1958.

Buckley, Vincent. *Poetry and Morality.* London: Chatto and Windus, 1959.

Chalker, John. 'Authority and Personality in Eliot's Criticism'. *Eliot in Perspective,* ed. Graham Martin. London: Macmillan, 1970.

Cruttwell, P. *The Shakespearean Moment.* London: Chatto and Windus, 1954.

Empson, William. *The Structure of Complex Words.* London: Chatto and Windus, 1951.

Engelmann, Paul. *Letters from Ludwig Wittengenstein*. Oxford: Blackwell, 1967.

Esterson, Aaron. *The Leaves of Spring*. London: Tavistock, 1970.

Frye, Northrop. *T. S. Eliot*. Edinburgh: Oliver and Boyd, 1963.

Goldberg, S. L. *The Classical Temper: A Study of James Joyce's Ulysses*. London: Chatto and Windus, 1963.

—. *An Essay on King Lear*. London: Cambridge University Press, 1974.

Gomme, Andor. *Attitudes to Criticism*. Carbondale: Southern Illinois University Press, 1966.

Grierson, Sir H. *Metaphysical Lyrics and Poems of the Seventeenth Century*. London: Oxford University Press, 1924.

Grigson, Geoffrey. 'Leavis against Eliot', *Encounter*, 16 (April 1959), pp. 68–9.

Harding, D. W. *Experience into Words*. London: Chatto and Windus, 1963.

—. 'T. S. Eliot, 1925–1935'. *Scrutiny*, v (1936–7), pp. 171–6; *and* xi (1942–3), pp. 60–7. Cambridge: Cambridge University Press, 1963 reprint.

Hartman, Geoffrey. *The Unmediated Vision*. New York: Harcourt, Brace, 1954. (Reprint with preface, 1966.)

van Heerikhuizen, F. W. (tr. Fernand Renier and Anne Cliff). *Rainer Maria Rilke, His Life and Work*. London: Routledge and Kegan Paul, 1951.

Heller, Erich. *The Poet's Self and the Poem*. London: Athlone Press, 1976.

Hough, Graham. *The Last Romantics*. London: Duckworth, 1949.

Howarth, Herbert. *Notes on some Figures behind T. S. Eliot*. London: Chatto and Windus, 1965.

Hudson, Liam. *Contrary Imaginations*. Harmondsworth: Penguin, 1966.

Hulme, T. E. *Speculations*. London: Routledge, 1965.

Johnson, Samuel, *Selected Works*. ed. Mona Wilson. London: Rupert Hart-Davis, 1950.

Kazin, Alfred. *Contemporaries*. London: Secker and Warburg, 1963.

Keats, John. *Letters of John Keats*. Selected by Frederick Page. London: Oxford University Press, 1954.

Kenner, Hugh. *The Invisible Poet*. London: Methuen, 1965.

Kermode, Frank. *Romantic Image*. London: Routledge and Kegan Paul, 1957.

—. *Selected Prose of T. S. Eliot*. Ed., with an introduction. London: Faber and Faber, 1975.

—. and (ed.) Hollander, J. *The Oxford Anthology of English Literature*, Vol. 6. Oxford: Oxford University Press, 1973.

Knights, L. C. 'Bacon and Dissociation of Sensibility'. *Explorations*. London: Chatto and Windus, 1946.

Kojecky, Roger. *T. S. Eliot's Social Criticism*. London: Faber and Faber, 1971.

Krieger, Murray. *The New Apologists for Poetry*. Minneapolis: University of Minnesota Press, 1956.

Laing, R. D. *The Divided Self: An Existential Study in Sanity and Madness*. Harmondsworth: Penguin Books, 1965.

—. *Self and Others*. London: Tavistock Publications, 1961.

—. *The Politics of Experience* and *The Bird of Paradise*. Harmondsworth: Penguin Books, 1967.

Langbaum, Robert. *The Poetry of Experience: the dramatic monologue in the modern literary tradition*. London: Faber and Faber, 1957.

Lawrence, D. H. 'Review' of *Georgian Poetry*, in *Selected Literary Criticism*, ed. Anthony Beal. London: Heinemann, 1956.

Leavis, F. R. *New Bearings in English Poetry*. London: Chatto and Windus, 1932.

—. *The Common Pursuit*. London: Chatto and Windus, 1952.

—. 'T. S. Eliot's Stature as a Critic'. *Commentary*, xxvi (1958), pp. 399–410; reprinted in *Anna Karenina and Other Essays*. London: Chatto and Windus, 1967.

— and Leavis, Q. D. 'Eliot's Classical Standing'. *Lectures in America*. London: Chatto and Windus, 1969.

Leavis, F. R. 'Eliot's "Axe to Grind" ', and the Nature of Great Criticism'. *English Literature in Our Time and the University*. London: Chatto and Windus, 1969.

—. *The Living Principle*. London: Chatto and Windus, 1975.

—. 'Mutually Necessary', *Universities Quarterly*, 30 (Spring 1976), pp. 129–51.

Lemon, Lee T. *The Partial Critics*. London: Oxford University Press, 1965.

Lewis, Wyndham. *Men Without Art*. New York: Russell and Russell, 1964. (Reprint of 1934 original).

Litz, Walton A. (ed.) *Eliot in his Time*, Princeton: Princeton University Press, 1973.

MacMurray, John. *Persons in Relation: Being the Gifford Lectures delivered in the University of Glasgow in 1954*. London: Faber and Faber, 1961.

Margolis, John D. *T. S. Eliot's Intellectual Development: 1922–1939*. Chicago: Chicago University Press, 1972.

Matthiessen, F. O. *The Achievement of T. S. Eliot*. Rev. ed. by C. L. Barber. New York: Oxford University Press, 1958.

Monod, Jacques. *Chance and Necessity*. London: Collins, 1972.

Montale, Eugenio. *Poems*. Selected and translated by George Kay. Edinburgh: Edinburgh University Press, 1964.

Newton-de Molina, D. (ed.) *The Literary Criticism of T. S. Eliot*. London: Athlone Press, 1977.

Nott, Kathleen. *The Emperor's Clothes. An attack on the dogmatic orthodoxy of T. S. Eliot, Graham Greene, Dorothy L. Sayers, C. S. Lewis and others*. London: Heinemann, 1953.

Patterson, Gertrude. *T. S. Eliot: Fragments into Poems*. Manchester: Manchester University Press, 1971.

Parkinson, Thomas. ' "Intimate and Personal": aspects of modern poetics'. *Journal of Aesthetics and Art Criticism*, 16 (1958), pp. 373–83.

Praz, Mario. 'T. S. Eliot and Dante', *The Southern Review*, 2 (Winter 1937), pp. 525–48.

Rajan, B. (ed.) *T. S. Eliot: a Study of his Writings by Several Hands*. London: Dennis Dobson, 1947.

Ransom, John Crowe. *The New Criticism*. Norfolk: New Directions, 1941.

Read, Sir Herbert. *Collected Essays in Literary Criticism*. London: Faber and Faber, 1962.

Rees, Sir Richard. *Brave Men: D. H. Lawrence and Simone Weil*. London: Gollancz, 1958.

Richards, I. A. *The Principles of Literary Criticism*. London: Kegan Paul and Co., 1929.

Ricks, Christopher. 'Review' of Leavis' *The Living Principle*. *Essays in Criticism*, xxvi (1976), pp. 363–70.

Rilke, Rainer Maria. *Sonnets to Orpheus* and *Duino Elegies*. Tr. J. B. Leishman. London: The Hogarth Press, 1936, 1948.

Robinson, Ian. *The Survival of English*. London: Cambridge University Press, 1973.

Robson, W. W. 'Eliot's Later Criticism', *The Review*, 1 (1962), pp. 52–8.

—. *Critical Essays*. London: Routledge and Kegan Paul, 1966.

—. 'Playing one Poem off against Another'. Review of Leavis' *The Living Principle*. *The Times Higher Education Supplement*, 3 October 1975, p. 14.

Santayana, George. *Selected Critical Writings*. Ed. Norman Henfrey. London: Cambridge University Press, 1968.

Sen, Jyoti Prakash. *The Progress of T. S. Eliot as Poet and Critic*. New Delhi: Longman-Orient, 1971.

Smidt, Kristian. *Poetry and Belief in the Works of T. S. Eliot*. London: Routledge and Kegan Paul, 1967.

Smith, Grover. *T. S. Eliot's Poetry and Plays*. Chicago: University Press, 1956.

Smith, James. 'Notes on the Criticism of T. S. Eliot', *Essays in Criticism*, xxii (1972).

Spender, Stephen. *The Destructive Element*, London: Jonathan Cape, 1935.

—. *Eliot*. London: Collins (Fontana Modern Masters), 1975.

Sprat, Thomas. *The History of the Royal Society of London*. Ed. Jackson L. Cope and Harold Whitmore Jones. London: Routledge and Kegan Paul, 1959.

Stead, C. K. *The New Poetic: Yeats to Eliot*. Harmondsworth: Penguin Books, 1967.

Thompson, Eric. 'Dissociation of Sensibility', *Essays in Criticism*, 2 (1952), pp. 207–13.

—. *T. S. Eliot—The Metaphysical Perspective*. Carbondale: Southern Illinois University Press, 1963.

Trilling, Lionel. *The Opposing Self*. London: Secker and Warburg, 1955.

—. (ed.) *Literary Criticism: an introductory reader*. New York: Holt, Reinhart and Winston, 1970.

—. *Sincerity and Authenticity*. London: Oxford University Press, 1972.

Unamuno, Miguel de. *The Tragic Sense of Life*. Tr. by J. Crawford Flitch. London: Macmillan, 1912.

Unger, Leonard (ed.) *T. S. Eliot: A Selected Critique*. New York: Russell and Russell, 1966.

Vivante, Leone. *English Poetry* (Introduction by T. S. Eliot). London: Faber and Faber, 1950.

Vivas, Eliseo. *Creation and Discovery*. New York: Noonday Press, 1955.

Ward, David. *T. S. Eliot: Between Two Worlds*. London: Routledge and Kegan Paul, 1973.

Watson, George. *The Literary Critics*. Harmondsworth: Penguin Books, 1973.

Watson, James B. and Crick, Frances. *The Double Helix*. Harmondsworth: Penguin Books. 1969.

Weil, Simone. *Waiting on God*. London: Collins, 1959.

—. *Selected Essays*. Tr. by Richard Rees. London: Oxford University Press, 1962.

—. *Science, Necessity and the Love of God*. London: Routledge and Kegan Paul, 1966.

Weiss, T. 'T. S. Eliot and the Courtyard Revolution', *Sewanee Review*, 54 (1946), pp. 289–307.

Whistler, James McNeill. *The Gentle Art of Making Enemies*. London: Macmillan, 1890.

Williams, Raymond. *Culture and Society, 1780–1950*. London: Chatto and Windus, 1958.

Wilson, Edmund. *Axel's Castle. A Study in the Imaginative Literature of 1870–1930*. London: Collins (Fontana Edition), 1961.

Wimsatt, W. K. *The Prose Style of Samuel Johnson*. New Haven: Yale University Press, 1941.

—. and Beardsley, Monroe. 'The Intentionalist Fallacy', *Sewanee Review*, 54 (1946), pp. 468–87.

—. and Brooks, Cleanth. *Literary Criticism: a short History*. London: Routledge and Kegan Paul, 1957.

Winkler, R. O. C. 'Crumbs from the Banquet'. *Scrutiny*, x (1941–2), pp. 194–8. Cambridge: Cambridge University Press, 1963 reprint.

Winters, Yvor. *In Defense of Reason*. New York: Swallow and William Morrow, 1947.

Wollheim, Richard. 'Eliot and F. H. Bradley: an account', *Eliot in Perspective* Ed. Graham Martin. London: Macmillan, 1970.

Yeats, W. B. *Essays and Introductions*. London: Macmillan, 1961.

NOTES

Prefatory: Eliot's Four 'Theories'

1 F. W. Bateson, 'Criticism's Lost Leader', *The Literary Criticism of T. S. Eliot*, ed. David Newton-de Molina (London, Athlone Press, 1977), p. 10.
2 Eric Thompson, *T. S. Eliot, The Metaphysical Perspective* (Carbondale, Southern Illinois University Press, 1963), p. 52.
3 F. W. Bateson, op. cit., p. 10.
4 Kristian Smidt, *Poetry and Belief in the Works of T. S. Eliot* (London: Routledge and Kegan Paul, 1967), p. 52.
5 Eric Thompson, op. cit., p. 53.
6 *The Sacred Wood*, pp. 14–15.
7 'The Metaphysical Poets', *Selected Essays*, pp. 287–8.
8 'Tradition and the Individual Talent', *Selected Essays*, pp. 17–18.
9 Ibid., p. 15.
10 Which gives a quite different impression to the notion of life as a 'skinning' —Gourmont's *la vie est un dépouillement*, which Eliot quotes with approval. That is reductive; perhaps even masochistic.
11 Eliot himself, it is only fair to say, did not use the word 'theory' here; but others have.
12 'Hamlet', *Selected Essays*, p. 145.
13 See the remarks on Behaviourism in the essay on John Bramhall, *Selected Essays*, p. 357.
14 'Nicoló Macchiavelli', the *Times Literary Supplement*, 16 June 1927, p. 413. Quoted in Mowbray Allen, *T. S. Eliot's Impersonal Theory of Poetry* (Lewisburg, Bucknell University Press, 1974).
15 'The Pensées of Pascal', *Selected Essays*, p. 367.

1. Critical Responsibility and Critical Approach

1 '. . . the word "impersonal" introduces a critical topic of the first importance.' F. R. Leavis, 'Thought and Emotional Quality', *Scrutiny*, xiii, 1945, p. 53.
2 See, as just one example, Jyoti Prakash Sen, *The Progress of T. S. Eliot as Poet and Critic* (New Delhi, Orient-Longman, 1971).
3 The uncompleted contest between F. R. Leavis and Eliot is the finest example of this, from *New Bearings in English Poetry* (1938) to *The Living Principle* (1975).
4 James Smith, 'Notes on the Criticism of T. S. Eliot', *Essays in Criticism*, xxii (Oct. 1972), pp. 333 ff.

5 It occurs in the essay on John Bramhall.

6 This word makes it seem as if what follows comes from 'Tradition and the Individual Talent'; in fact it is from 'Imperfect Critics' in *The Sacred Wood*, p. 32.

7 In an obituary notice in the same edition of *Essays in Criticism* (op. cit., p. 447 ff.) F. W. Bateson, sympathetic to 'Tradition and the Individual Talent', describes this essay as 'perhaps the very best article this journal has produced in its . . . life'.

8 'Tradition and the Individual Talent', p. 21.

9 op. cit., p. 17.

10 F. W. Bateson, ' "Impersonality" Fifty Years After', *Essays in Critical Dissent* (London, Longman, 1972), p. 156.

11 Bateson, op. cit., p. 157. The phrase 'a conduit of urgent life', is Leavis', from his essay on Eliot as a critic. Bateson says of it (p. 156) that it 'is intended, I suppose, to emphasize the writer's personality as the self-sufficient medium for the communication of "life" '. That isn't fairly put, for the context is: '. . . one can be as free as D. H. Lawrence was from any romantic inclination to say that the artist's business is to "express his personality" . . . and still . . . believe as intensely as Lawrence did that without the distinguished individual . . . there is no art that matters'. Leavis has said that Eliot was one such individual. Leavis' view of personality is the challenge to Eliot's; and the form of it would be that Lawrence was himself impersonal in an utterly different way. (See particularly: 'Lawrence After Thirty Years', an address given at Nottingham University, 1960; reprinted in H. Coombes (ed.), *D. H. Lawrence* (Penguin, 1973).

12 Michael Black, 'That Which is Perfectly Ourselves', *The Human World*, No. 6, February 1972, pp. 4–5. Black is speaking of *Phèdre*. Eliot is, to a degree, just such a profound negative voice: it is implied in his 'classicism'.

13 'Tradition and the Individual Talent', *Selected Essays*, p. 18.

14 op. cit., p. 20.

15 op. cit., p. 17. [Eliot] 'contributes to the modern suspicion of criticism that relates a writer's work to his life'. J. D. Margolis, *T. S. Eliot's Intellectual Development* (Chicago, Chicago University Press, 1972), p. xiii.

16 Sir Herbert Read's essay, 'The Personality of the Poet', *Collected Essays in Literary Criticism* (London, Faber, 1962), pp. 21–40, attempts to answer Eliot by bringing in psychology: 'We cannot hope to arrive at a definition of personality without encroaching to some extent on a science of psychology.' He has Freud particularly in mind. Eliot seems to be referring to this essay in a footnote to *The Use of Poetry and the Use of Criticism*, where he remarks that Read's argument takes him 'where I would not willingly follow'.

17 *The Use of Poetry and the Use of Criticism* (London, Faber, 1933), p. 84.

18 F. W. van Heerikhuizen, *Rainer Maria Rilke, His Life and Work*, tr. Fernand Reiner and Anne Cliff (London, Routledge, 1951. Dutch ed. 1946). See Preface, pp. x–xi, and: 'He who wants to see Rilke must be able to stand outside him after having interpenetrated him' (p. 381). An injunction for our aproach to Eliot.

19 Yvor Winters, *In Defense of Reason* (New York, Swallow and William Morrow, 1947), p. 460.

20 John Crowe Ransom, 'The Historical Critic', *The New Criticism* (Norfolk, New Directions, 1941), pp. 135-8.

21 The argument over the value of philosophy to literary criticism is not one I want to enter into here. I will only refer to the exchanges between René Wellek and F. R. Leavis—see F. R. Leavis, *The Common Pursuit* (Harmondsworth, Peregrine Books, 1962), pp. 211-22. The argument is renewed in *Universities Quarterly*, 30 (Spring 1976), pp. 129-51.

22 Eliseo Vivas, 'The Objective Correlative of T. S. Eliot', *Creation and Discovery* (New York, Noonday Press, 1955), pp. 175-89.

23 Vincent Buckley, *Poetry and Morality* (London, Chatto and Windus, 1959), p. 108.

24 'Preface to *Lyrical Ballads*'.

25 'The Metaphysical Poets', *Selected Essays*, p. 287.

26 Thomas Parkinson, 'Intimate and Impersonal: aspects of modern poetics', *Journal of Aesthetics and Art Criticism*, 16 (March 1958), p. 373.

27 *Selected Essays*, p. 19.

28 John Chalker, 'Authority and Personality in Eliot's Criticism' in *Eliot in Perspective*, ed. Graham Martin (London, Macmillan, 1970), p. 194.

29 T. S. Eliot, 'The Frontiers of Criticism', *On Poetry and Poets* (London, Faber and Faber, 1965), p. 106.

30 Miguel de Unamuno, *The Tragic Sense of Life*, tr. J. Crawford Flitch (London, Macmillan, 1912), p. 2.

31 C. K. Stead, *The New Poetic, Yeats to Eliot* (London, Penguin Books, 1967), p. 131 fn.

32 Buckley, op. cit., p. 96.

33 Stead, op. cit., p. 129. The three essays to which Stead refers are those on Jonson, *Hamlet*, and 'Tradition and the Individual Talent'.

34 See above, p. 12, and below, pp. 66, 67 and 123.

35 Kristian Smidt, op. cit., p. 52.

36 One can see the act of entry into the specialist-methodological version here: 'I would argue that we do not need a justificatory ontology, nor a speculative quasi-logical ontology, but a scientific ontology; that is to say an ontology founded on a carefully controlled concept derived from appropriate sciences and generating a wide range of descriptive terms available to critics with many different interests in the study of many different kinds of texts.' How fine must the mesh be before nothing gets away? Roger Fowler, 'The Structure of Criticism and the Languages of Poetry' in *Contemporary Criticism*, ed. Malcolm Bradbury (London, Edward Arnold, 1970), pp. 175-6.

37 F. R. Leavis, 'Eliot as Critic', *Anna Karenina and Other Essays* (London, Chatto and Windus, 1969), pp. 177-8.

38 Richard Wollheim, 'Eliot and F. H. Bradley: an account' in *Eliot in Perspective*, ed. Graham Martin, p. 190.

39 On this see again Leavis, op. cit., and W. W. Robson, 'Eliot's Later Criticism', *The Review*, 1 (1962), pp. 52-8.

40 *The Use of Poetry and the Use of Criticism*, p. 35.

41 C. K. Stead, op. cit., p. 126.

42 C. K. Stead, op. cit., p. 126. See also his remark: '... that separation of functions against which the whole effort of the best contemporary poetry and criticism has been directed'. (p. 192).

43 As E. M. Forster's *Howards End*, with its epigraph '... only connect', exemplifies disconnection.

44 '*Hamlet*', *Selected Essays*, pp. 143–4.

45 See F. W. Bateson, on bibliography, in 'The Philistinism of Research', *Essays in Critical Dissent*', pp. 1–15.

46 Paul Engelmann, *Letters from Ludwig Wittgenstein* (Oxford, Blackwell, 1967), p. 5.

11. Impersonality: 'Sacrifice' or 'Extinction'?

1 See W. W. Robson, 'Playing one poem off against another', *Times Higher Education Supplement*, No. 206, 3 Oct. 1975, p. 14.

2 Geoffrey Grigson, on Leavis' essay on Eliot as a critic, first published in *Commentary*, xxvi, 1955, pp. 399–410. Grigson's remarks, part of a deplorably *personal* attack on Leavis, appeared as 'Leavis against Eliot' in *Encounter*, 16 (April 1959), pp. 68–9.

3 Thomas Sprat, *History of the Royal Society of London* (1667), ed. Jackson L. Cope and Harold Whitmore Jones (London, Routledge and Kegan Paul, 1959), pp. 111–13.

4 George Watson, *The Literary Critics* (Harmondsworth, 1973), p. 172. Perhaps only odd to modern historians.

5 Introduction to 'Tradition and the Individual Talent' in *Oxford Anthology of English Literature*, ed. F. Kermode and J. Hollander, vol. 6 (Oxford, Oxford University Press, 1973), p. 2013.

6 F. R. Leavis, 'Literature and Society' in *The Common Pursuit*, pp. 183–4.

7 D. W. Harding, 'T. S. Eliot, 1925–1935', *Scrutiny*, v (1936–7), pp. 171–6 and also *Scrutiny*, xi (1942–3), pp. 60–7 (Cambridge, Cambridge University Press, 1963, reprint).

8 Stephen Spender, *The Destructive Element* (London, Jonathan Cape, 1935), p. 161.

9 'Johnson as Critic and Poet', *On Poetry and Poets*, p. 165.

10 'Authority and Personality in Eliot's Criticism', op. cit., p. 194.

11 Samuel Johnson, 'Preface to Shakespeare', *Prose and Poetry*, ed. Mona Wilson (London, Rupert Hart-Davis, 1957), p. 489.

12 'Authority and Personality in Eliot's Criticism', *Eliot in Perspective*, ed. Graham Martin (London, Macmillan, 1970), p. 194.

13 From 'Seneca in Elizabethan Translation', *Selected Essays*, p. 75.

14 'That which is read with admiration in the pages of Johnson, may be discovered with amusement in the imitations of his immediate successors, but the further the imitation is protracted by posterity, the greater must be the danger that the effort will excite but a murmur of polite disgust, or a smile of frigid indifference.' W. K. Wimsatt (parodistically), *The Prose Style of Samuel Johnson* (New Haven, Yale University Press, 1941), p. 148.

15 *After Strange Gods*, pp. 54–5.

16 I make use of a term from the psychiatrist Gregory Bateson. See Bateson
   et al.: 'Towards a theory of schizophrenia', *Behavioural Science*, i, 251.
17 *Selected Essays*, pp. 424–5.
18 R. D. Laing, *The Divided Self* (London, Penguin Books, 1965), p. 19.
19 September–October 1919 (misdated 1917 in many editions of *Selected Essays*).
20 F. W. Bateson, ' "Impersonality" Fifty Years After', *Essays in Critical
   Dissent* (London, Longman, 1972), p. 153.
21 'In his criticism of authors Eliot makes numerous judgements, frequently
   without any attempt to substantiate them . . . the question is not the validity
   of these judgements, but Eliot's method of presenting them': Allen Austin,
   T. S. Eliot, The Literary and Social Criticism (Indiana University Press, Bloomington, Indiana, 1971).
22 The confident justification of art by reference to science is very much of the
   general spirit of this period: see Hulme's *Speculations*, and parts of de Gourmont. On occasion it becomes a tactic, to *épater* the conventional: 'Other
   people paint localities; Mr Whistler makes artistic experiments.' (See James)
   McNeill Whistler, *The Gentle Art of Making Enemies* (London, 1890), p. 126.
23 I don't mean to suggest that Eliot did not recognise these things in himself.
   See *Lines* for Cuscuscaraway and Mirza Murad Ali Beg: 'How unpleasant to
   meet Mr. Eliot: With his features of clerical cut . . .' (*Collected Poems*, p. 147).
24 R. O. C. Winkler, *Scrutiny*, x, 1941 (Cambridge University Press reprint,
   1963), p. 195. Why, furthermore, should Winkler associate *empiricism* with a
   'lack of logic'? It is as if he thought that empiricism was *eclectic*—piecemeal
   in its approach.
25 But then: *Quis custodiet scientiam ipsam?* 'At bottom the ideal of literary
   scholarship that Greg and McKerrow and their associates have incarnated has,
   I suppose, been an unconscious tribute to the physical sciences. The closer the
   literary "fact" could be reduced to a physical "thing" the more effective
   their methods became.' F. W. Bateson, '*Cui Bono?* A Learned Journal's
   Irrelevance', *Essays in Critical Dissent*, p. 61.
26 It is this that makes Eliot's later way of discussing the matter, in 'The Three
   Voices of Poetry', *On Poetry and Poets*, pp. 97–8, so much better, so much
   'more intimately felt' as W. W. Robson puts it in his *Critical Essays*.
27 'The Three Voices of Poetry', *On Poetry and Poets*, p. 98. What Eliot tries to
   do in part II of 'Tradition' isn't so far from this, and on a grander scale.
28 'I have used similitudes.' Hosea xii, 10: the epigraph to *The Pilgrim's Progress*.
29 Stephen Spender does not notice this change. Of the crucial passages in part I
   of 'Tradition' he says: 'This picture of tradition as a *system* like a *functioning
   mechanism* can . . . not . . . be taken seriously as a *scientific working model* . . .
   Eliot is not making a blueprint, diagrammatically explaining the relation
   between the tradition and the creativity of the contemporary artist, in the
   manner of a model of the structure in a science museum . . .' (*my italics*). In
   this part of the essay there is no attempt to rest upon scientific vocabulary in
   that way. Eliot is not doing what Mr Spender says he is—and is not—doing.
   Stephen Spender, *Eliot* (Collins, Fontana 'Modern Masters', 1975), p. 75.
30 'The Function of Criticism', *Selected Essays*, p. 27. G. S. Fraser in a comparison of Eliot with Yeats says that Eliot could often be 'mean, snobbish

and uncharitable', see Neville Braybrooke ed., *T. S. Eliot, a symposium for his 70th birthday* (London, Rupert Hart-Davis, 1958).

31 See Robert Langbaum, *The Poetry of Experience* (London, Faber, 1957). And A. L. French, 'Purposive Imitation', *Essays in Criticism*, 1972.

32 This is a very strange association of the devouring and of the inert, is it not —of the passive with the active? Do receptacles *seize*? Can one catch one's fingers in one's own metaphor? It may be that the affinity of the word with 'tentacle' (i.e. 'tentacular roots' in the essay on Ben Jonson, *Selected Essays*, p. 155) has led Eliot to a rhyme.

33 *Selected Essays*, p. 19.

34 W. K. Wimsatt and Monroe Beardsley, 'The Intentionalist Fallacy' (*The Sewanee Review*, 54, 1946), p. 470.

35 And again, though the intention is different: '. . . you can hardly say that Shakespeare believed, or did not believe, the mixed and muddled scepticism of the Renaissance. If Shakespeare had written according to a better philosophy, he would have written worse poetry . . .' ('Shakespeare and the Stoicism of Seneca', *Selected Essays*, p. 137). Putting aside the question of how you might 'believe' scepticism (it is easier to imagine believing a muddle or part of a muddle), and the shift between 'believe' and 'write according to', still—how does Eliot *know* what Shakespeare 'would have written'?

36 Stead, *The New Poetic*, p. 127.

37 'Eliot does not say whether this intensity of the artistic process is a function of the inert mind of the poet or an accident affecting the mind from without . . . Nor, if we try to interpret the figure . . . can we determine what is meant by inertness of intensity; nor can we guess what occurs when the poet writes: the entire process is a mystery, and if the critic can say no more about it than he has said, he would have done well to employ less and simpler language.' Yvor Winters, 'T. S. Eliot, or the Illusion of Reaction', *In Defense of Reason* (New York, Swallow and William Morrow, 1947), p. 466. One would want to say that it is not a matter of less and simpler language, but of a different language that would turn out to be simpler.

38 Eliot creates many of these: thought-feeling, man-poet, tradition-talent, mind-emotion, blood-brain, orthodoxy-heresy. There is a constant tendecy to set one thing against another (not as co-operative) and then to see them as if they were real entities or elements; to hypostatize them, and thus make them more difficult to reconcile.

39 At this point there is a confusing shift in the argument from creation to effect, on to the person who enjoys it. The 'it' could refer to the effect rather than 'the work of art'.

40 Stead, *The New Poetic*, p. 129.

41 To emphasize the point once more: Stead, like Winkler earlier, works as does Eliot inside the same set of analytic–classifying assumptions.

42 Vincent Buckley, *Poetry and Morality* (London, Chatto and Windus, 1959), p. 105.

43 F. W. Bateson, 'Dissociation of Sensibility', *Essays in Critical Dissent*, p. 145.

44 'The struggle to come to terms with, to deal intelligently with, an emotion so deeply felt as Wordsworth's, must involve an activity which is dialectical.

Wordsworth achieves a balance . . .' Vincent Buckley, *Poetry and Morality*, p. 175.

45 'It is easy to see why, in a chaotic world, Leavis should consider a certain impersonality, a certain detachment, necessary, if an inner development is to take place in the individual. It needs great reliance on one's personal judgment . . . if a man is not to sink under the weight of chaos in the world.' Vincent Buckley, op. cit., p. 188.

46 *Selected Essays*, p. 21.

47 A 'common language judgment' occurs when 'the weight of the language' is for, or against certain expressions; 'the weight of the common values, we create merely by speaking English'. Ian Robinson, *The Survival of English* (Cambridge University Press, 1973), p. 13.

48 Eliot bridled himself sharply when it came to poetry. His *Collected Poems* give the impression of someone who wrote little, and perhaps with difficulty; but he is in fact reputed to have written a great deal, and thrown a great deal away.

49 'Johnson as Critic and Poet', *On Poetry and Poets*, p. 191.

50 Andor Gomme, *Attitudes to Criticism* (Carbondale, Southern Illinois University Press, 1966), p. 134.

III. Personality and the Proper Relation

1 Mildred Martin, *A Half-Century of Eliot Criticism. An Annotated Bibliography of Books and Articles in English 1916–1965.* (Lewisburg, Bucknell University Press, 1972.)

2 I have not been able to find any; but non-findings are inconclusive. See Mowbray Allan, *T. S. Eliot's Impersonal Theory of Poetry* (Lewisburg, Bucknell University Press, 1972), for a chapter on Eliot's attitude towards personality.

3 Owen Barfield, *Saving the Appearances, A Study in Idolatry* (New York, Harcourt, Brace and World, n.d.), p. 89. The book he refers to is L.-B. Geiger, *La Participation dans la Philosophie de S. Thomas d'Aquin* (Paris, 1942?)

4 This occurs in Eliot himself: 'Sometimes a critic may choose an author to criticize, a role to assume, as far as possible the antithesis to himself, a personality which has actualized all that has been suppressed in himself; we can sometimes arrive at a very satisfactory intimacy with our anti-masks.' *The Use of Poetry and the Use of Criticism*, p. 112.

5 D. H. Lawrence, review in *Rhythm* (March 1913) of *Georgian Poetry: 1911–1912*, reprinted in *Selected Literary Criticism*, ed. Anthony Beal (London, Heinemann, 1956), p. 72.

6 T. E. Hulme, *Speculations* (London, Routledge and Kegan Paul, 1936; reprint 1965), p. 33.

7 John Macmurray, *Persons in Relation* (London, Faber and Faber, 1961), p. 34.

8 Miguel de Unamuno, *The Tragic Sense of Life*, translated by J. Crawford Flitch (London, Macmillan, 1912), p. 8.

9 ibid.

10 *The Destructive Element* (London, Jonathan Cape, 1935), p. 159.

11 C. K. Stead, *The New Poetic*, p. 131.

12 See T. W. Baldwin, *Shakespeare's small Latin and lesse Greeke* (Urbana, Illinois University Press, 1944).

13 *The Use of Poetry and the Use of Criticism*, p. 35. This and the footnote come from a note 'On the Development of Taste in Poetry' added to the Introduction.

14 ibid., p. 35.

15 There is a parallel in the conclusion of 'From Poe to Valéry' in *To Criticize the Critic*, p. 42. (See below, pp. 84–5.)

16 'Thomas Middleton', *Selected Essays*, p. 161.

17 And, of course: '. . . a great artist or artisan of the Elizabethan epoch'. 'Thomas Middleton', *Selected Essays*, p. 162.

18 I owe this point to Professor W. W. Robson.

19 'Thomas Middleton', *Selected Essays*, p. 161.

20 'Philip Massinger', *The Sacred Wood*, pp. 133–4.

21 'Ben Jonson', op. cit., p. 118. 'Transfusion' comes from de Gourmont, in roundabout, or echoic, ways: *transvaser goutte à goutte*.

22 'Imperfect Critics', op. cit., p. 29, p. 32. This quotation is the context for the phrase cited by James Smith (see above, p. 12) and shows how unfair the remark is to Eliot. In context it means almost the opposite of what is made of it. But Eliot makes it too easy.

23 'Philip Massinger', *The Sacred Wood*, p. 134.

24 op. cit., p. 143.

25 'Tradition and the Individual Talent', *Selected Essays*, pp. 19–20.

26 Eliot, of course, frequently sees the need for relation: 'Wyndham forgets . . . that . . . it is not, in the end, periods and traditions but individual men who write great prose. For Wyndham himself is a period and a tradition.' 'Imperfect Critics', *The Sacred Wood*, p. 29.

27 It is remarkable how relatively little Eliot has to say about Shakespeare, and the *nature* of his greatness. For that see Patrick Cruttwell, *The Shakespearean Moment* (London, 1954).

28 C. K. Stead, *The New Poetic*, p. 14.

29 F. R. Leavis, *Lectures in America* (London, Chatto and Windus, 1969), p. 5

30 'Philip Massinger', *The Sacred Wood*, p. 123.

31 'Splitting or "doubling" himself into languid sufferer and satiric commentator he [Laforgue] wrote poems deriding in one passage the tendencies of another. Eliot accommodated this idiosyncrasy to his own needs; it helped him veil personal agonies with impersonal ironies.' Grover Smith, *T. S. Eliot's Poetry and Plays* (Chicago, Chicago University Press, 1956), p. 5.

32 'Philip Massinger', p. 124.

33 W. B. Yeats, *Essays and Introductions* (London, Macmillan, 1961), p. 266. Yeats also makes a conjunction that Eliot does not: '. . . we have lost in personality, in our delight in the whole man.'

34 'Imperfect Critics', *The Sacred Wood*, p. 23.

35 'Andrew Marvell' and 'The Metaphysical Poets', *Selected Essays*, pp. 304, 287, 288.

36 See Sir Herbert Butterfield, *The Origins of Modern Science 1300–1800* (London, Bell, 1949), p. 104.

37 'The Perfect Critic', *The Sacred Wood*, pp. 1–2.

38 A fuller collection (of the kind given under Note A at the end of this chapter) might precipitate this kind of judgment: '[the] terms are suspiciously scientific. What with "prisms", "elements" . . . a character's "nature" seems a rather fixed and static thing, as though it were merely one, definably "individualized" element in the author's vision'. S. L. Goldberg (of Arthur Sewell's *Character and Society in Shakespeare*), *An Essay on King Lear* (London, Cambridge University Press, 1974), p. 46.

39 'The Perfect Critic', *The Sacred Wood*, p. 12.

40 See the precise parallel in the remark of S. L. Bethell, below p. 145 on Basil Willey's statement that: 'I think that something of the peculiar quality of the "metaphysical" mind is due to this fact of its not being *finally committed* to any one world. Instead, it could hold them all in a loose synthesis together . . .' (*The Seventeenth Century Background*, p. 43).

41 There is, of course, another paradox here. There is general agreement that the quality of the earlier criticism is higher than the later. Again, part of the explanation may lie in the connection between intensity and unfulfilled wholeness.

42 'The Perfect Critic', *The Sacred Wood*, p. 13.

43 But in a rather equivocal way. See his introduction to *The Need for Roots* (London, Routledge and Kegan Paul, 1952).

44 See Simone Weil, *Science, Necessity and the Love of God*, ed. Richard Rees (London, Oxford University Press, 1966).

45 'The Perfect Critic', *The Sacred Wood*, pp. 9–10.

46 Something of the possible connection between 'objectification' (the defence against 'personality' in the bad sense) and the 'theories' is brought out here: 'Pound's idea of poetry as a "sort of inspired mathematics which gives us equations, not for abstract figures, triangles, spheres, and the like, but for the human emotions", may be the starting point for Eliot's theory of the "objective correlative"'. Mario Praz, 'T. S. Eliot and Dante', *The Southern Review*, Vol. 2, No. 3, pp. 525–48. One of the connections is metaphorical, as here, where the figurative language is drawn—how consciously?—from the scientific 'register'.

47 'The Metaphysical Poets', *Selected Essays*, pp. 287, 288.

48 ibid.

49 In *Explorations* (London, Chatto and Windus, 1946), p. 111.

50 op. cit., p. 111.

51 See F. O. Matthiessen, *The Achievement of T. S. Eliot*, rev. ed. by C. L. Barber (New York, Oxford University Press, 1956), for remarks on the 'conspicuous lack of reference to Chaucer'. It should however be added that Dante was a very current presence in North American high culture, in a way that Chaucer was not. See Martin Green, *The Problem of Boston*.

52 'Dante', *Selected Essays*, pp. 237–77, and 'What Dante Means to Me' in *To Criticize the Critic*, pp. 125–35. There are of course many passing references, as there are to Shakespeare.

53 See 'Donne in Our Time' in *A Garland for John Donne*, ed. T. Spencer (Cambridge, Harvard University Press, 1931), p. 8.

54 'The Metaphysical Poets', *Selected Essays*, p. 283.

55 Frank Kermode, *Romantic Image* (London, Routledge and Kegan Paul, 1957), pp. 140–4.

56 See above, p. 34.

57 L. C. Knights, op. cit., p. 109.

58 From a note to Chapter IV of *The Use of Poetry and the Use of Criticism*: 'On Mr Herbert Read's appraisal of Wordsworth', pp. 84–5.

59 I would like to mention here (partly as a defence of what may at first seem an exaggerated introduction of this psychological term) a use of it by Eliot himself in *The Use of Poetry and the Use of Criticism*. Speaking of the relation between poetry and philosophy he says that:

> I believe that for a poet to be a philosopher he would have to be virtually two men; I cannot think of any example of this thorough schizophrenia, nor can I see anything to be gained by it: the work is better performed inside two skulls than one. Coleridge is the apparent example, but I believe that he was only able to exercise the one faculty at the expense of the other . . . (pp. 98–9)

One will bear in mind here Eliot's own philosophical training . . . a personal parallel to the historical parallel: schizophrenia *is* a splitting; Eliot speaks of the splitting of personality in English Literature, of dissociation of sensibility; and schizophrenia is a derangement. But Eliot does not make these connections explicit. One can only *assume* that they are clear to him. It is also well worth noting that this must be a very early use of the word 'schizophrenia' in a non-clinical, popular, or at least general sense, only twenty years after it was coined (1911) by Bleuler to characterize that 'core problem of insanity' which involves the assumption of separate characters or roles. Previous uses are botanical or zoological: 'schizogenic'. (See the *Encyclopædia of the Social Sciences*.) Eliot had the most painful personal reasons for acquaintance with the term.

60 'From Poe to Valéry', *To Criticize the Critic*, p. 42.

61 *Notes towards the Definition of Culture*, p. 19.

62 'Eliot is provocative; his general statements are sufficiently pertinent and wise to compel thought, but cryptic and undeveloped enough to permit his would-be disciples to set out in diverse and even opposite directions. Moreover, he has a habit of making apparently forceful statements, then qualifying the last drop of meaning from them.' Lee T. Lemon, *The Partial Critics* (London, Oxford University Press, 1965), p. 36.

63 Richard Wollheim, 'Eliot and F. H. Bradley: an account' in *Eliot in Perspective*, ed. Graham Martin (London, Macmillan, 1970), p. 185.

64 *Knowledge and Experience in the Philosophy of F. H. Bradley* (London, Faber and Faber, 1964).

65 Wollheim, op. cit., pp. 186–7.

66 'To Criticize the Critic', *To Criticize the Critic*, pp. 19–20.

67 op. cit., p. 20.

68 op. cit., p. 19.

69 *The Use of Poetry and the Use of Criticism*, p. 77.

70 The idea of the 'objective correlative' is subtly linked with this; as perhaps is this:

> Andrewes' emotion is purely contemplative; it is not personal, it is wholly evoked by the object of contemplation, to which it is adequate; his emotion is wholly contained in and explained by its object . . . Donne is a 'personality' in a sense in which Andrewes is not . . . Andrewes is wholly absorbed . . . [he] has the *Gout pour la vie spirituelle*.

> ('For Lancelot Andrewes', *Selected Essays*, p. 351.)

71 Wollheim, op. cit., p. 173. Something of the pressure of the historical need can be gathered from this: 'The Spanish landscape . . . carried this attitude of mine to its extreme limits: for there the outward things themselves . . . instantly possessed the . . . unsurpassable intensity of the inner equivalents . . . Appearance and vision everywhere merged in the object, in each a whole interior world was revealed, as though an angel who encompassed all space were blind and gazing into himself.' (Rilke, letter to Ellen Delp, 1915.) The 'object' is actually nothing at all, but a metaphysical 'point' where inner and outer meet.

72 *The Use of Poetry and the Use of Criticism*, p. 76.

73 'The Possibility of Poetic Drama', *The Sacred Wood*, p. 64.

74 *Notes Towards the Definition of Culture*, p. 20.

75 *The Use of Poetry and the Use of Criticism*, p. 88.

76 op. cit., p. 101. The letter is in *Letters of John Keats*, selected by Frederick Page (Oxford, 1954), p. 48.

77 See Erich Heller, *The Poet's Self and the Poem* (London, 1976), where he speaks of Rilke's 'mere saying' ('Dinge Gedichte'): 'A detachment so complete is now required of the artist that . . . a century and a half of self-consciousness and a great deal of "history" have sufficed to make what after all is only a new variation on "negative capability", sound so harsh and extreme that Keats . . . would hardly have recognized it.'

78 This is the root of Eliot's quarrel with Lawrence, who went in the Romantic direction. See the latter's comment on 'all this classiosity'.

79 *Letters of John Keats*, ed. cit., pp. 354–5. 'Godwin-methodist' might be translated today as 'technologico-Benthamite'. And the word 'method' there, has its implications for all our 'methodologists'.

80 *The Use of Poetry and the Use of Criticism*, p. 100.

81 Lionel Trilling, *The Opposing Self* (London, Secker and Warburg, 1955), p. 37.

82 *The Use of Poetry and the Use of Criticism*, p. 102.

83 *Letters of John Keats*, ed. cit., p. 53.

84 *The Use of Poetry and the Use of Criticism*, p. 162.

85 The word 'identity' was available to him; Keats uses it in his letters, expressing a necessary distinction which is part of the intention of Eliot's 'impersonality'.

86 'Yeats', *On Poetry and Poets*, p. 255. The essay itself dates from 1940.

87 'Four Elizabethan Dramatists', *Selected Essays*, p. 114.

88 Kristian Smidt, *Poetry and Belief in the Works of T. S. Eliot*.

89 Allen Austin, *T. S. Eliot, The Literary and Social Criticism*. See pp. 6–7.

90 *The Use of Poetry and the Use of Criticism*, p. 85.

91 op. cit., p. 119. Arnold's letters, incidentally are remarkable for quotations, and the repetition of quotations. Touchstones, or supports? Or—since Rilke asked in one of his letters 'What is a prayer?' perhaps something even more? Consider the part played in Eliot's writings by quotation. Cf. Chapter IV, n. 10.

92 Neville Braybrooke ed., *T. S. Eliot, a symposium for his 70th birthday*.

93 See W. W. Robson, reviewing *The Living Principle*, by F. R. Leavis, *The Times Higher Education Supplement*, 3 Oct. 1975, p. 14: 'Leavis is . . . determined to see Eliot not only as a great poet but as a "case" . . .'

94 D. W. Harding, 'T. S. Eliot, 1925–1935', *Scrutiny*, xi (1942–1943), pp. 60–7.

95 Lionel Trilling, *Sincerity and Authenticity* (London, Oxford University Press, 1972), pp. 6–7.

96 W. M. Wimsatt and Cleanth Brooks, *Literary Criticism: A Short History* (London, Routledge and Kegan Paul, 1957), p. 662.

97 ibid., p. 662.

98 'The Music of Poetry', *On Poetry and Poets*, p. 32.

99 'The Dry Salvages', V.

100 'Little Gidding', I.

101 Lionel Trilling, *Sincerity and Authenticity*, pp. 7–8.

102 'Paradoxical communications are mystifying in that they tend to engender confusion over an issue, rather than conflict.' Aaron Esterson, *The Leaves of Spring* (London, Tavistock Publications, 1970), Penguin edition, 1972, p. 253.

iv. Conclusion: Self and Society

1 'Johnson as Critic and Poet', *On Poetry and Poets*, pp. 165–6. Eliot's sense of 'other things' is expressed by him in his essay on Marvell in this way: 'a recognition, implicit in the expression of every experience, of other kinds of experience which are possible' (*Selected Essays*, p. 303).

2 See the remarks of R. D. Laing on the difficulty for the healthily whole personality of understanding schizophrenia. *The Divided Self*, p. 8.

3 Geoffrey Hartman, *The Unmediated Vision* (New York, Harcourt, Brace and World, 1954), p. 164.

4 Geoffrey Hartman, op. cit., p. 168.

5 See pp. 36–7, 58–63. It seems to be general knowledge that Eliot would not permit the reprinting of this collection during his lifetime.

6 'Ash Wednesday', *Collected Poems, 1909–1935*, p. 93.

7 'Marina', *Collected Poems, 1909–1935*, p. 114.

8 See, as one example of this attitude, James Watson and Frances Crick, *The Double Helix* (on the structure of DNA) (Harmondsworth, Penguin Books, 1969). Another example, of many, would be, Jacques Monod, *Chance and Necessity* (London, Collins, 1972).

9 F. R. Leavis' term. See *The Living Principle* (London, Chatto and Windus, 1975), p. 55.

10 This word will perhaps not seem too strong if we consider the intensity of his interest in certain authors (and the 'conversion' of other authors to suit that interest) and the extraordinary intuition of his quotation. We remember

those quotations so well, that we may assume that we needed them, too. People do have these needs, and do read to give them outlet. Consider this remark by Simone Weil: 'In reading, as in other things, I have always striven to practise obedience . . . as far as possible I only read what I am hungry for, at the moment when I have an appetite for it, and then I do not read, I eat' (*Waiting on God*, Collins (Fontana edition), 1959, p. 36). Consider too this remark of M. C. Bradbrook's: 'They are more than "happy quotations" in the usual sense: frequently they constitute Eliot's main statement . . . Hence the strength with which they stamp themselves on the mind of the reader, and the frequency with which they pass into general circulation' ('Eliot's Critical Method' in B. Rajan ed., *T. S. Eliot: A Study of his Writing by Several Hands* (London, Dennis Dobson, 1947), p. 124). And Eliot himself: 'If we are moved by a poem it has meant something, perhaps something important, for us; if we are not moved, then it is, as poetry, meaningless' ('The Music of Poetry', *On Poetry and Poets*, p. 30). Eliot also speaks of 'the craving for poetry' which develops 'at or about puberty' and which continues with some people throughout life (*The Use of Poetry and the Use of Criticism*, p. 30). Once again: 'an intellectual interest is not enough'.

11 'To Criticize the Critic', *To Criticize the Critic*, pp. 16–17. This remark would only be interesting if Eliot were to note the extent of such 'conditioning' as unusual—and then try to explain *why* his present criticism is so different.

12 It was perhaps the recognition of this which led to Leavis' *Revaluation*.

13 F. W. van Heerikhuizen, *Rainer Maria Rilke: his Life and Work*, tr. Fernand Renier and Anne Cliff (London, Routledge and Kegan Paul, 1951), pp. 13–14. Heerikhuizen also quotes the following (p. 17) which is worth showing again because of its close parallel to Eliot's remarks above (cf. p. 80 above) on the proliferation of knowledge:

> Modern man carries within him an enormous number of indigestible knowledge-stones that occasionally rattle together in his body, as the fairy-tale puts it. And the rattle signifies the most striking characteristic of this modern man, the opposition of something within him to which nothing external corresponds; and the reverse. The ancient nations knew nothing of this. Knowledge, taken in excess without hunger, even contrary to desire, no longer has the effect of transforming the internal life; and remains hidden in a chaotic inner world that modern man takes a curious pride in calling his 'real personality'.
> Friedrich Nietzsche: *Von Nützen und Nachteil der Historie für das Leben* (On the Advantage and Disadvantage of History to Life).

14
> Penso che per i piu non sia salvezza
> ma taluno sovverto ogni disegno
> passi il varto, qual volle si
> ritrovi.

(I think that most are not to be saved / but someone overturns every plan / wins through the gaps, finds what he wanted.) Eugenio Montale, 'Casa sul Mare', *Selected Poems*, tr. George Kay (Edinburgh, Edinburgh University Press, 1964). (A number of critics have drawn parallels between Montale and Eliot.)

15 Heerikhuizen, op. cit., p. 307.
16 F. R. Leavis, *Lectures in America* (London, Chatto and Windus, 1969), p. 30.
17 Heerikhuizen, op. cit., p. 8.
18 Wyndham Lewis, *Men Without Art*, 1934 (New York, Russell and Russell re-issue, 1964), p. 74.
19 Kathleen Nott, *The Emperor's Clothes* (London, Heinemann, 1953), p. 221.
20 ibid.
21 'La science ne possède aucune valeur ordonnatrice' (André Malraux).
22 Hugh Kenner, *The Invisible Poet* (London, Methuen, 1965), p. 96. The quotation comes from Eliot's 1919 review of *The Education of Henry Adams*. Another 'discharge'?
23 I am reluctant to pass by the recollection of the oddly similar title of a poem by Robert Bly: 'After the Industrial Revolution, All Things Happen at Once.'
24 T. S. Eliot, *Knowledge and Experience in the Philosophy of F. H. Bradley*, p. 30. See also Gertrude Patterson, *Fragments into Poems*, p. 5, and note following:
    'From the monist Bradley . . . Eliot derived certain assumptions about the nature of experience . . . Reflected in Eliot's work is Bradley's view of the personality as a mere cluster of imperfections and delusions.' Grover Smith, *T. S. Eliot's Poetry and Plays* (Chicago, Chicago University Press, 1956), p. 4.
25 '. . . the unending attrition of human sensibility, caused by the deadly machinery of the age is countered by the poetic self's . . . withdrawal that T. S. Eliot went so far as to call "extinction of personality".' Erich Heller, *The Poet's Self and the Poem*, p. 72.
26 Gertrude Patterson, op. cit., p. 3. And 'Just as Bradley defined reality of an object as the sum of its individual appearances, so Eliot's generality, his comprehensiveness, is made up by assembling particular observations, personal views.' (p. 11).
27 Rilke to his Polish translator in 1925. Quoted in J. B. Leishman tr., *Sonnets to Orpheus* (Hogarth Press, 1936), p. 19.
28 Hugh Kenner, *The Invisible Poet*, p. 41.
29 ibid., p. 39.
30 Sir Herbert Grierson, Introduction to *Metaphysical Lyrics and Poems of the Seventeenth Century* (Oxford, Oxford University Press, 1924), p. 3.
31 'The Social Function of Poetry', *On Poetry and Poets*, p. 25.
32 Frank Kermode's comment that 'Somehow, and probably soon, the age of dissociation—which is to say, the age that invented and developed the concept of dissociation—must end', does not seem likely to be fulfilled—at least, not soon. *Romantic Image*, p. 160.
33 Walter Jackson Bate, *The Burden of the Past and the English Poet* (London, Chatto and Windus, 1971), pp. 133–4.
34 'The Social Function of Poetry', *On Poetry and Poets*, p. 25.
35 Yvor Winters, 'T. S. Eliot: the Illusion of Reaction', *In Defense of Reason* (New York, Swallow and William Morrow, 1947), p. 500.
36 If Leavis on the one hand speaks of the necessity of the intensity of inner 'need' to the creation of the *Four Quartets* and *Ash Wednesday* (see 'Eliots

Classical Standing' in *Lectures in America*, as well as *The Living Principle*) then
to have 'escaped' from the prison of the need and to have finally affirmed
human creativity would have meant that we—and he—would not have had
the poetry as it is. We can't be sure, any more than Eliot could have been,
that we would have had anything; or anything comparably fine. Leavis, for
all the wonderful attentiveness—truthfulness—of his criticism, is drawn into
this paradox, by speaking as if he is not fully aware of it. It is a matter of tone.
There are worse dangers, however, in being *too* aware of it.

37 This appears to be the judgment made by Christopher Ricks in his review of
The Living Principle (the Dantesque section of *Little Gidding* is being referred
to):

> ... Leavis wonderfully elicits the distinction of the famous passage, and
> yet his praise of it is importantly evasive. Eliot has been imprisoned in a
> frustrating self-contradiction, 'Yet in this magnificent passage he comes
> near to escaping'. What exactly is it, in such a case, to come near to escap-
> ing? And that it may be Leavis who is coming near to escaping from his
> own stringencies becomes clear when two paragraphs later 'near to escap-
> ing' has unobtrusively become something crucially different: 'what Eliot
> achieves ... is a momentary escape from the prison'. 'A liberating flash',
> a 'genuine and liberating impersonality'. Is Eliot liberated or not? ... the
> imprisonment seems to be Leavis's, ruled for the moment by the ruling
> idea which has mostly elicited the truth of the poem but which at this vital
> point is insufficient or at any rate insufficiently argued for. *Essays in
> Criticism*, xxvi (Oct. 1976); pp.363–70.

I say 'appears to be' because I am not so sure what Professor Ricks wants:
that Eliot should be allowed to have escaped from the prison *permanently*?
Even if that were so it would not mean that he could tell himself that he had
'always been committed to creativity'.

38 S. L. Bethell, *The Cultural Revolution of the XVII Century* (London, Dennis
Dobson, 1953), pp. 98–9.

39 ibid. (My italics.)

40 F. R. Leavis (see *Lectures in America*, pp. 31–2 and 37–9) does *not* make a
distinction between the quality of the two parts of 'Tradition and the
Individual Talent'.

41 Simone Weil, 'Human Personality', *Selected Essays*, p. 26.

42 Alfred Kazin, *Contemporaries* (London, Secker and Warburg, 1963), p. 15.

43 George Santayana, 'Three Philosophical Poets', *Selected Critical Writings*, ed.
Norman Henfrey (Cambridge, Cambridge University Press, 1968), pp.
146–56. (Santayana uses words like *Truth* and *Good* with a freedom quite
alien to modern criticism and philosophy.)

44 In 1934, for example, he wrote that: 'I do not repudiate what I wrote in that
essay any more fully than I should expect to do after such a lapse of time.'
After Strange Gods, p. 15. Another example of giving and taking.

45 'The Metaphysical Poets', *Selected Essays*, p. 287.

46 *After Strange Gods*, p. 26.

47 R. D. Laing, *The Divided Self*, p. 37.

48 'If I had undertaken a SYSTEMATIC defence of the theory here maintained ...'

Although science is in the background of the essay, Wordsworth does not claim its principles for what he is doing. Eliot is not systematic, in this sense, ever.

49 *After Strange Gods*, p. 11.

50 '. . . it may be this lurking sense of not quite belonging, not quite fitting, of having put on ill-fitting, second-rate ideas like an ill-fitting, second-rate world, will be part of Eliot's claim to the semi-permanent modernity of a classic.' Robert M. Adams, 'Precipitating Eliot', *Eliot in his Time*, ed. A. Walton Litz, p. 153.

51 Simone Weil, 'Human Personality', *Selected Essays*, pp. 13-14.

INDEX

Note. As the book itself is fairly short, and as the Notes can be scanned to find references in the text, this Index has been restricted to a *list* of some of the main uses of the recurrent 'key words' associated with an enquiry into the words 'personality', 'impersonality', 'theory' and 'self', which themselves occur *passim.*